Prayer Zone Workout

Spiritual and Physical Exercise for the Heart

Rachel Britton

TO THE MEMORY OF
my mother
Patricia Elizabeth Mullender

"Acquire the habit of speaking to God as though you were alone with God. Speak with familiarity and confidence as to your dearest and most loving friend. Speak of your life, your plans, your troubles and joys, your fears. In return, God will speak to you – not that you will hear audible words in your ears, but words that you will clearly understand in your heart."

attributed to Alphonsus Liquori
(1696-1787)

Contents

Foreword

This book does a wonderful job of inviting people to engage in cultivating the habits of the heart through the practice of prayer. Along with the companion app, *Prayer Zone Workout* is a unique contribution to those who long to grow deep in the life of prayer, thus strengthening the heart for and toward God. I very much appreciated the journal entries, which were quite honest and powerful in content and appropriately organized based on the theme of each chapter. Also, the tone of the book draws curious readers to not only read the words, but to actively jump into the practice of prayer. Prayer Zone Workout is a wonderful contribution to those who want to live their lives in the presence of God, who is with us and is for us!

Dr. S. Steve Kang
Professor of Educational Ministries & Interdisciplinary Studies
Gordon-Conwell Theological Seminary

Chapter 1
Discovering Prayer

Exercise daily in God—no spiritual flabbiness, please! Workouts in the gymnasium are useful, but a disciplined life in God is far more so, making you fit both today and forever. You can count on this. Take it to heart. This is why we've thrown ourselves into this venture so totally.
1 Timothy 4:7-10 (MSG)

"Your assignment," Professor Lee spoke softly and calmly, "is to spend one to two hours each day in individual, personal prayer." Though his demeanor was tranquil, he stated this goal with firm conviction, as though two hours of prayer were as crucial for our existence as food and water. I wondered what the other twenty-nine students in this week-long class, The Practice of Prayer, were thinking now.

My thoughts turned to my own prayer life. I found practicing daily prayer—especially for extended periods of time—quite difficult. My mind frequently wandered. Other matters jostled for attention in my head, declaring their importance. My prayers seemed long, but a glance at the clock would tell me otherwise. Only a few minutes had passed, and I would become disillusioned with my superficial efforts.

There were times when I managed consistent, if somewhat short, prayer time—maybe ten minutes each morning for a few weeks—until, inevitably, my routine would get disrupted. During an especially busy week or school vacation, this practice would disappear altogether. Then the challenge would be getting back into my routine once things returned to normal. And so my personal prayer time would wax and wane like the moon.

Still, I wanted to pray better, to learn how to master my own practice of prayer. This was one of the reasons I chose The Practice of Prayer as part of my seminary degree, and why I now sat in the classroom listening intently to Professor Lee. I longed to establish a consistent and regular prayer time that would be forever woven into the fabric of my day. I yearned to stay focused. I wanted to be motivated, not frustrated. These desires stirred deep within me. If I worked diligently during the week-long class, then perhaps I could satisfy these needs. I hoped the result would be more than selfish gratification. Sincere prayer, I believed, would open the way to positive inner change, which in turn would evidence itself in an outward constructive reality.

My week was filled with many hours in the practice of prayer. In the classroom we practiced silent, individual prayer in short five or ten-minute bursts, as directed by Dr. Lee. But our homework each evening was to spend one to two hours in *continuous* prayer. Some days, as soon as class finished, I drove to an isolated spot in the parking lot and spent an hour or more praying in my car. After spending six hours in the classroom, I would open the car windows and doors to enjoy the fresh summertime air. Other times I might shut myself up with a large mug of tea in the basement of our home, the commotion of family life going on above me. My family was patient with these new routines. They were already used to my disappearing for hours at a time to read books and write papers at odd times of the day.

At first, spending more than one hour in personal prayer seemed a daunting task. Nevertheless, I resolved to make the effort and apply myself to the work. Reading lengthy theological books for other courses had already required me to take a disciplined approach to my studies, including dividing reading assignments into precise numbers of pages to be read each day. For The Practice of Prayer, I simply transferred this method from reading to praying. If I was following a five-step prayer instruction from the classroom session of that day, I broke down my prayer time at home into five manageable chunks. For an hour of prayer, I devoted twelve minutes, precisely, to each step. After twelve minutes I would move on to the next step. This way, I didn't lose concentration, and I began to experience success in reaching my goal.

Prayer, then, replaced the many hours of reading weighty books that had filled my time during other seminary courses. Praying, I found, was *light* compared to reading Kant or Nietzsche. Spending one to two hours in prayer each day became less difficult as time went on. I was gaining an appetite and a taste for prayer that I had not previously experienced.

I also sensed, as the week progressed, a greater spiritual dimension. Prayer no longer meant sterile, silently verbalized words, but instead became rich with meaning. It was *heart talk*. I was talking to God with my whole being—my mind, my emotions, and my spirit. The constant bombardment of "stuff" no longer distracted me. Instead, the stuff of my life spiraled up, like the smoke of incense, to God. I was listening to and hearing from God. I was getting his perspective on my heart talk, and learning more about who he is, who I was in his eyes, and how I should live. Finally, my prayers were deeper and longer conversations with God.

Previously I had barely considered the condition of my spiritual heart. But after reaching this new stage in my prayer life, I began to understand that my spiritual heart is the core of my being from which everything flows; the source of my thoughts, feelings, words and actions. Now, that spiritual heart took center stage. I sensed its beating, its rhythm, and I became aware of its condition. I started to disclose the contents of my heart to God, and I allowed it to be searched and illuminated by his Holy Spirit. This was like receiving a spiritual shower. I felt my heart being spiritually massaged to remove its muscle knots, becoming more pliable, softer, and healthier. Prayer was changing me on the inside.

But it did not stop there. The effects of this heart talk were also playing out in my daily life. Within a single week, the yearning I had for a consistent, motivating, and life-changing prayer-practice experience was gaining momentum.

The difficulty, of course, came when that week ended and the course concluded. Could I continue to stay committed to this practice of transformative personal prayer on my own?

IN THE ZONE:

What do you find hard about the practice of prayer? Is it difficult to be consistent, to get motivated, and to stay focused? Does your life seem too busy to fit in a regular prayer time? Perhaps, you find prayer boring.

In his book, *Prayer: Does It Make Any Difference?* Philip Yancey points out that prayer often ranks high in theoretical importance but low in actual satisfaction.[1] Is prayer unsatisfying for you? Maybe, you think of it as not productive—you don't see the results you want. Or, as Richard Foster says, perhaps you think you "have to have everything 'just right' in order to pray."[2]

Write down the difficulties you have with prayer that you would like to overcome:

Is this your experience with physical exercise, too? You know its value, but you just don't find it fulfilling; it's hard to do.

Write down difficulties you have with physical exercise that you would like to overcome:

Say this prayer: *Heavenly Father, these are the things I find difficult with prayer and exercise:* Read out your list to God. At the end add: *I want to make a commitment to overcome these difficulties. With you Lord, I can be successful. Amen.*

Congratulations! This is your first prayer towards a fitter and healthier you.

Don't be satisfied with "It's hard to practice." Instead, practice hard to be satisfied.

---

1   Philip Yancey, *Prayer: Does It Make Any Difference?* (Grand Rapids, Mich.: Zondervan, 2006), 15.
2   Richard Foster, Prayer - Finding The Heart's True Home (Hodder & Stoughton, 1993), 7.

Chapter 2
Scheduling Prayer

"Here's what I want you to do: Find a quiet, secluded place so
you won't be tempted to role-play before God. Just be there as
simply and honestly as you can manage. The focus will shift from
you to God, and you will begin to sense his grace.
Matthew 6:6 (MSG)

After awakening to my desire for the regular practice of prayer in my daily life, I thought about all the things that take up my time: juggling the many demands of work, raising a family of three teenagers, running a home, being present for my husband, taking rest and relaxation, and managing the injection of the unexpected into all of this. How could I possibly add the spiritual exercise of prayer into days that were already crowded? It seemed impossible.

Yet, I had already made daily walks or bike rides a priority in my busy schedule because I saw and felt the positive effect of regular exercise on my body and mind. It helped maintain my weight, toned my body, and brought relief when I was feeling stressed. The results of working out, along with a routine I enjoyed, motivated me to continue.

Perhaps, I thought, I could simply *combine* daily prayer and physical exercise. In that way I would be completing both activities in half the time it would take to accomplish each separately. I was, to be honest, concerned that the praying part might end up being a halfhearted effort tagged onto my physical exercise. It occurred to me that what I needed was a structured prayer routine that would fit with the shape of my physical exercise routine. I wanted physical exercise to *prompt* me to pray and for prayer to spur me on in my physical routine.

I considered my physical exercise program—core exercises, strength training using free weights, and aerobic exercise. The aerobic exercise is either a thirty-minute walk or a seven-to-ten mile bike ride. I cycle on a local path than runs through our suburban town along a disused railway

13

line. I walk at an outdoor track conveniently located only a few minutes' drive from our house. Years ago I carved out time for exercise in the early morning, and now it is as much a habit as my morning cup of tea. As soon as my children have left for school, I jump in my car and head to the track.

This six-lane, red, cushioned oval dominates a wide-open space surrounded by other recreational sites: tennis courts, a skate park, baseball fields, and swimming pools. The town's high school sits at one end, and this is where my twin boys attend school. When I arrive around 7:30 a.m., the area is already a hive of activity. Tennis partners play a game of doubles; dog owners walk their pets; runners and walkers loop the track, and some jog while waiting for the local bus that stops in the parking lot. Yet despite all this activity, the four things I need for the practice of prayer are present in this teeming place: rhythm, harmony, order and self-discipline.

Rhythm comes with the constant movement of footfalls, even though the cushioned track muffles, to some degree, the sound they might otherwise make. Runners sprint or jog, their staccato paces even and quick on the inside lanes. Those not as physically adept step more slowly, legato style, on the outside lanes. Although each individual moves independently, together they create a pattern: individual runners sounding out their patterns of daily exercise.

There is *harmony* created by people of all types—women and men, large or small, wearing fitness gear or regular clothes, conducting simple routines or more intricate exercise regimes—blending with one another in their commitment to physical fitness.

I was welcomed by a number of these people when I started coming regularly to the track. One was my next-door neighbor; two others were mothers with children the same age as my own; and another was an affable man called Abraham who loves to strike up a conversation. But most days we are silent, like-minded in our individual pursuits of physical well-being.

I experience *order* as walkers and runners flow counterclockwise around the track, with sprinters on the inside lanes and slower-paced walkers on the outside lanes. Sometimes an individual, oblivious to the directional flow of the group, chooses to walk clockwise, disrupting the rhythm and creating a disconcerting obstacle for the rest of us. High school students contribute briefly to this break in flow as they cut across the track, trying to make it on time to the start of school. But once they have gone, we settle comfortably back into our lanes.

I value the *self-discipline* demonstrated by members of the track community. Their routines are regular and consistent. They all take stretch breaks at the same point in their exercise sessions and at the same location every day. Runners always place their water bottles on the very end of the bleachers before starting their workouts. Most of us even park our cars in the same space each day. Through all these deeply etched habits, this community conveys a sense of tranquility through the orderly focus of mind, body, and spirit. This order only comes with self-discipline, the same kind of self-discipline that is also needed for a regular, extended practice of prayer.

IN THE ZONE:

Do you carve out time for regular exercise? Where do you go to exercise? To the gym? Riding through the neighborhood or on a bike trail? To a yoga class?

Make a list of places where you might be able to both exercise and pray. Choose a place that has spiritual elements that you believe will make it easier for you to experience prayer—perhaps a secluded path through the woods, on the beach, or somewhere with a view of the mountains. Even if you live in a city, can you think of a place close to where you live that will help bring you closer to God?

Will you enjoy visiting here? Make sure your answer to this question is yes, because if it is, then you are more likely to be successful with exercising and praying on a regular basis.

Finally, are you free from distractions in this location? This is important. For instance, walking in your neighborhood might not be the best place because you're likely to run into people you know who would divert you from your prayer time.

Make this enjoyable, distraction-free environment your special *go to* place. Write down the location for your Prayer Zone and list the things that make it the perfect spiritual place for you.

Find a sacred place to place yourself with the One who is sacred.

Chapter 3
Shaping Prayer

Our Father in heaven... Give us today our daily bread. And
forgive us our debts... deliver us from the evil one.
Matthew 6:9-13 (NIV)

The track in the center of town is my sacred space. There are other places I exercise, but this particular place allows me to feel close to God and makes it easier for me to pray. Since I was already working out regularly at the track, it made sense to incorporate a prayer routine into my daily walk. While my body was occupied with walking, my mind, I reasoned, would be free to focus on praying. The solitary nature of my exercise would allow me to spend time communicating with God. I began to see each lap as a chunk of manageable prayer time. My routine—warm-up, high-intensity, low-intensity and cool-down—was a natural fit for structured prayer.

I've always prepared my *body* for exercise with warm-up stretches, so stretching my mind to think about the content of my prayer each morning was a natural first step. Fortunately, it didn't take long for this mind-stretching to become a habit. Sometimes I'll focus on an attribute of God. Often my stretching involves thinking about events in my life or how I am feeling; other times I'm conscious of pressing concerns that may have arisen the previous day. During my stretching, I choose the things I am going to pray about—things that are burdening my spiritual heart—knowing how this load is lightened when I talk it over with God; it's rather like walking off a heavy meal. My stretching prepares me for a dedicated time to discuss and work out my life with God.

For my warm-up lap, I orient my mind and heart to be in God's presence. Usually, in the hubbub of our family morning life, I neglect to acknowledge God, even though I know he is present with me in the midst of my earthly activities. So warm-up for me is specifically designed to turn my thoughts to him. Exercising outdoors helps with this activity. I focus on God's creation—the light puffy or billowing clouds, the bright morning sun or the bone-chilling wind, the bare trees or golden leaves, robins hopping through the grass or geese squawking as they fly in formation overhead—nature reminds me of God's presence.

Once my mind is completely focused on God, I step up my walking to a brisk pace. This is when the high-impact part of my workout begins. I feel my heart rate increase, and I become aware of breathing more deeply. It is during these laps of more intense physical activity, that I talk to God about those pressing matters that are troubling me most. It's as if my spiritual heart pumps faster, too, as I bring my anger, hurt, and worries to God. I become so engrossed in off-loading these issues to God that before I know it, I have completed half a mile (two laps) or more. This is good heart-work, both physical and spiritual!

Next I transition to low-intensity walking, which gives my body a chance to recover. During these laps my pace is slower. Likewise, my spiritual heart slows down. Now it is time to redirect my mind and heart away from my troubles and toward listening to God. Sometimes a scripture verse comes to mind. Other times I comprehend a better perspective on my anger, hurt or worries. I realize that my anger is causing me to behave unkindly. I understand that I am worrying instead of trusting God. This is how I hear God's voice.

At any time during my workout, I may choose to speak to God again; during those times I return to my brisker walking pace. If I have sinned, I ask God for forgiveness. If I feel hurt, I ask him for healing. If I perceive his goodness, I thank him for all he has done for me.

This pattern repeats itself throughout my workout. My conversation with God becomes *interval training* for my soul as well as my body. I become aware that prayer, my spiritual exercise, helps me complete two miles of walking, my physical exercise. It feels good! Both my body and soul are becoming stronger.

Now I am ready to complete my workout with a cool-down lap to return my body to normal activity and prepare my spiritual heart for entering back into daily life. This cool-down is always a time to remember that I am not alone: God goes with me into my day. Sometimes, anticipating my day fills me with trepidation, so I ask God for his protection. Other times I imagine clothing myself with the spiritual armor that he provides so I am prepared to stand firm against temptations. And every day I ask God for his guidance, faith, hope and love so that I can live a life that is pleasing to him.

I step off the track thoroughly exercised and fully prepared for life.

Since that week when I sat in a classroom learning about The Practice of Prayer, I have created a physical and spiritual rhythm in my life. I am *hooked* on prayer. I am addicted—the best kind of addiction, of course—to both my physical exercise and my spiritual practice of prayer. My mind longs for time to breath. My body craves the routine. My spirit thirsts for its prayer workout, too. Mornings when I don't get to the track, I sense agitation in my mind, body and spirit. I can't wait to get there each day because this activity brings peace to my life.

My soul feels parched without prayer. Prayer: the water that brings refreshment to my soul.

My body lacks muscle tone without exercise. Exercise: the nourishment that brings strength to the body. The combination of exercise and prayer is oxygen that releases my mind to positive thinking. Through my Prayer Zone Workout, my body, mind and soul are renewed.

IN THE ZONE:

Now it's time for you to start devising your own personal Prayer Zone Workout plan. Fill in the blanks.

> Prayer Zone Workout Plan
> Location: _____
> You should have already decided on a location at the end of Chapter Two.
>
> Time: _____
> Choose a time of day that suits your schedule. It may be early in the morning, in the evening or even during your lunchtime at work.
>
> Duration: _____
> Decide how much time you can devote to a workout. If this seems overwhelming, start with 5 or 10 minutes.
>
> Days: _____
> Aim for five days a week, but choose any number of days that will help you be successful.
>
> Type of exercise: _____
> Walking, running, swimming, biking, even working out at the gym all fit comfortably within a Prayer Zone Workout. If you already have an exercise routine, consider turning it into a Prayer Zone Workout.

If you are just starting physical exercise, check with your physician before beginning any exercise regime.

Shaping your prayer helps satisfy your soul.

Chapter Four
Forming Healthy Habits

*Get away with me and you'll recover your life. I'll show you how
to take a real rest. Walk with me and work with me—watch how
I do it. Learn the unforced rhythms of grace. I won't lay anything
heavy or ill-fitting on you. Keep company with me and you'll
learn to live freely and lightly."*
Matthew 11:28-30 (MSG)

Having the *desire* to pray and exercise does not necessarily lead to us *practicing* prayer and physical activity. The step between wanting and doing can be like a chasm we do not know how to cross.

In Chapter One, I spoke of my own frustration with not being able to practice prayer on a regular basis. I would begin with enthusiasm and the goal of having a daily prayer time only to fail a few weeks later in achieving this objective. Yet now, as I said in the previous chapter, *I have created a physical and spiritual rhythm in my life. I am hooked on prayer. I am addicted—the best kind of addiction, of course—to both my physical exercise and my spiritual practice of prayer.* How did this happen? In this chapter we will explore the science of habits.

Maybe you want your own experience to change from one of failure to success. You have said, "I'm going to start exercising," or "I'm going to have a more regular prayer time." Perhaps you manage these pursuits for a while, but then your routines are disrupted by other circumstances in your life. Yet when life returns to normal, you find it hard to pick up where you left off and grow the habits you had hoped to acquire. Or your new routines work well until life becomes stressful, and then your prayer and exercise fall by the wayside.

So, how do you turn good intentions into healthy habits? How can you make the activities of prayer and exercise a part of your life so they are automatically included rather than excluded, regardless of what happens in your day?

Understanding how habits are formed and how they function can help you move from this start-stop treadmill to consistency of purpose in forming healthy prayer and exercise habits.

Scientists at Massachusetts Institute of Technology in Boston have discovered that habit-forming takes place in a part of the brain called the basal ganglia.[1] These researchers describe a *habit* as "a neurological loop consisting of a *cue*, a *routine* and a *reward*."[2]

The cue is a trigger that tells your brain to perform the routine. For a Prayer Zone Workout routine, my cue is to put on my fitness attire the moment I get out of bed in the morning. Wearing a sports top and shorts is my signal for action, to get to the track as soon as possible. Your cues may be anything that is regular and meaningful for pointing you to your chosen form of physical exercise.

My cue for the routine of prayer is stepping onto the track. As I start to walk, I am prompted to begin praying. My mind and heart focus on God and having conversation with him. Yours may be straddling your bicycle, stepping out your front door to start your run, or checking in at the desk in

---

1   "How the Brain Controls Our Habits," *MIT News*, accessed September 28, 2014, http://newsoffice.mit.edu/2012/understanding-how-brains-control-our-habits-1029.

2   Charles Duhigg, *The Power of Habit: Why We Do What We Do in Life and Business*, Reprint edition (Random House, 2012), 422.

the gym. The point is to have something that you consciously and consistently associate with beginning your prayer time.

After your cue the next part of the habit loop is to establish a *routine*. The routine is a physical, mental or emotional behavior that is repeated on a regular basis.[3] A Prayer Zone Workout routine includes all three aspects of behavior. It consists of physical exercise, and prayer that uses the mind and involves the emotions. In addition, a Prayer Zone Workout incorporates the spiritual practice of meditation, and speaking and listening to God, too.

Finally, the routine leads to the *reward*. The reward is the benefit gained from the behavior. After completing two miles at the track, my reward is physical, mental and emotional. I feel good, I am less stressed, I sleep better, and my body becomes more toned. Another reward is when the physical activity I initially found difficult becomes easier, and I am able to increase the duration and intensity of my workouts.

The reward from prayer is spiritual, mental, and emotional. I feel calmer after bringing my anxieties to God and meditating on his truths. I may receive clarity on a problem, or appreciate the opportunity to ask for and receive forgiveness. However, I am not only dependent on rewards resulting from my behavior. I receive spiritual assurance from God that by praying I am doing God's will.

In addition to receiving physical, mental, emotional and spiritual benefits from a Prayer Zone Workout routine, surprisingly, I also experience financial rewards. By recording my physical activity using the Run-Keeper fitness app on my cell phone, I earn points with Walgreens, which transfer into monetary savings.

When we experience rewards, it is easier to repeat the routine the next time we are prompted by a cue. This helps form the habit. Over time, the *cue—routine—reward* loop becomes automatic because the brain, constantly looking for ways to save effort and become more efficient, converts a sequence of actions into an automatic behavior. This process is called *chunking*.[4] Once these actions are automatic, the habit is formed, and it

---

3   Ibid., 423.
4   Ibid., 392.

becomes a positive part of the rhythm of our lives.

In addition to the habit loop becoming automatic, the brain creates neurological cravings that drive the loop. Once the habit is developed, the brain anticipates the reward, and it creates a craving for the reward. As we associate cues with particular rewards, a subconscious craving emerges.[5] If I don't get to the track for my workout, then I don't get my reward and I experience a craving for feeling good—a release of the endorphins from my exercise, and peace from spending time with God. I feel unsettled until I have satisfied my craving. Cues not only trigger the routine, but they can also trigger the craving. Cravings—positive cravings—spur on good habits.

At the beginning of this chapter, I said that our new routines of prayer and exercise often work well until we hit a stressful period in our lives, even though we already know they can help reduce stress. When that happens we lose the drive to persist in these activities. Researchers have discovered that faith, whether it is in God, a higher power, or something else, helps people navigate through stressful periods and make a habit a permanent behavior.[6] Therefore, since a Prayer Zone Workout incorporates belief and the practice of praying to God with the practice of physical exercise, you should be encouraged that it is even more possible for you to turn healthy habits of prayer and exercise into permanent behaviors.

In addition, habits are formed more easily with a group of people than on your own. When you see the change in someone else, you can believe that you too are capable of changing. Community creates belief.[7]

Finally, just as the prayer I experienced at seminary set off my determination to develop the healthy habit of prayer and exercise in my life, I hope the second half of this book will give you the determination to build your Prayer Zone Workout habit.

---

5   Ibid., 846.
6   Ibid., 1384.
7   Ibid., 1396–7.

IN THE ZONE

Write down some cues you think might work for you as you try to form a Prayer Zone Workout habit. Then select one and try it out. If it does not work, try out another cue. Do not give up – keep experimenting to find the right cue. When you have found one that works, share what it is and why it works for you with other people at www.facebook.com/prayerzoneworkout.

For your prayer and exercise routine, dream big but set realistic goals. If you set a goal that is too high and you fail to achieve it, you might be less likely to try again the next time. But don't give up. Alter it. Make it fit your life. Set yourself up for success.

Write down some achievable and realistic goals for your Prayer Zone Workout. To help you, I have made the first workout only 20 minutes long, even though 35 minutes is ideal for a Prayer Zone Workout. Start slowly. Small victories will convince you that larger accomplishments are achievable.

In later chapters you will be encouraged to journal about your activities, goals and rewards. Journaling about your rewards will encourage you to continue.

Get together a group of friends and share your achievements to encourage each other.

Use prayer as a cue for exercise and exercise as a cue for prayer

Chapter 5
Creating Heart-talk

Create in me a pure heart, O God, and renew a steadfast spirit within me. Psalm 51:10 (NIV)

We want prayer to become a healthy habit, *and* we hope our prayers will be deep and meaningful so they will impact our lives and the lives of those around us. Sometimes our prayers can seem empty of meaning and emotion, like thoughts from the top of our heads. We engage deeply in prayer when our thoughts move from our minds to dwell in our hearts, when they flow from the depths of our being. From there our thoughts form words rich with significance and fertile with purpose instead of being barren and pointless.

Scripture describes the heart as the center of our being. The heart is essentially our whole being—the core of who we are—and it governs our lives.[1] The heart, also referred to as the inner nature, is at the center of what you say, do and think. Not surprisingly, God is not so concerned with our outward appearance, with which we are so often obsessed; rather he observes, searches, and examines our hearts. If God pays attention to our hearts, then when our prayer is heart talk, he takes notice. We want to pray heartfelt prayers.

How do you know when you are praying with your heart? If the heart is our whole being, then when we pray with our heart it must involve our mind, will, emotions and body. When you pray with emotion, understanding, and purpose, then I believe you can say you are praying with your heart.

One of the first times I realized I was praying with my heart I began to cry. My mind understood that I had been neglecting my relationship with God up until then and that I needed to change. But through God's grace, the thought moved from my mind to my heart, because it flowed from my

---

1   Howard Marshall et al., eds., *New Bible Dictionary*, 3rd ed. (InterVarsity Press, 1996), 456.

spirit.

The biblical character of Hannah is a good example of someone who prayed with her heart. The book of Samuel says Hannah *prayed in her heart* so fervently that Eli, the priest in the temple, thought she was drunk! But Hannah explained she had not been pouring wine into her body to drown her sorrows; instead, she had been pouring out her anguish, from *the center of her being*, to God.[2]

In a Prayer Zone Workout we want our prayers to be from our heart because it is through this type of prayer that our lives are made healthier from the inside out. Oswald Chambers says: "Prayer is not a matter of changing things externally, but one of working miracles in a person's inner nature."[3]

Rich, fertile prayer involves our whole being—our mind, emotions, and spirit, and like rich fertile soil it *will* bear fruit. The theologian and author Richard Foster describes prayer as "a path whereby our lives can be taken over by love and joy and peace and patience and kindness and goodness and faithfulness and gentleness and self-control."[4] This list of attributes contains the fruits of the Spirit described in Galatians 5:22-23.[5] They flow from the heart into our lives and the lives of those around us. Prayer, therefore, has the potential to improve the fitness of your heart and make your life healthier.

The starting point of your heart talk is when your spiritual heart is changed from a "heart of stone" to a heart of flesh. We all have hearts of stone until we are broken, humbled, and penitent before God. At this point, our hearts of stone are crushed. Scripture says *your heart-shattered life doesn't for a*

---

2   1 Samuel 1:13-15 (NIV): Hannah was praying in her heart, and her lips were moving but her voice was not heard. Eli thought she was drunk and said to her, "How long are you going to stay drunk? Put away your wine." "Not so, my lord," Hannah replied, "I am a woman who is deeply troubled. I have not been drinking wine or beer; I was pouring out my soul to the Lord."

3   Oswald Chambers, *My Utmost for His Highest: An Updated Edition in Today's Language: The Golden Book of Oswald Chambers* (Grand Rapids, Mich.: Discovery House, 1992), sec. August 28.

4   Richard Foster, *Prayer: Finding The Heart's True Home* (Hodder & Stoughton, 1993), 5.

5   Galatians 5:22-23a: But the fruit of the Spirit is love, joy, peace, forbearance, kindness, goodness, faithfulness, gentleness and self-control.

moment escape God's notice.[6] God replaces your crushed stone heart with a new heart of flesh beating with his Spirit. You can care for the health of your new heart through prayer. Prayer enables you to work at loving God with all our heart, soul, mind, and strength, and loving other people, too. *Prayer* is your spiritual workout!

For these reasons, the heart is at the center of the practice of prayer *and* exercise in a Prayer Zone Workout. Combining prayer and exercise is not just a convenient way to make the most of our time; it also helps us connect having a healthy physical heart with a having a healthy spiritual heart. When we concentrate on both simultaneously, our praying reminds us to take care of our "temple of the Holy Spirit," while our exercising acts as a prompt for the habit of regular prayer. When we do both at the same time, we are taking care of both kinds of "heart."

Aerobic exercise is cardiovascular: it strengthens the physical heart and makes it work more efficiently. Aerobic exercise also leads to other health benefits such as improving the muscles' consumption of oxygen and their ability to burn fat.[7] Therefore, aerobic exercise is vital for our physical health. It also enables us to involve our physical bodies in the spiritual activity of prayer. In this way we really are using our whole beings when we pray.

Kneeling and lifting or folding our hands are the most familiar ways we use the physical body in prayer. These postures are physical manifestations of the reverence for God we hold in our hearts. In scripture David *danced before the Lord with all his might*[8] (much to the disgust of his wife).[9] In a Prayer Zone Workout we are engaging the body in prayer through walking, jogging, or another aerobic activity.

I believe the most significant component of our heart talk is that it connects us with the Eternal. Scripture tells us God has set eternity in the

---

6   Psalm 51:16-17 (MSG)

7   "Aerobic Exercise Symptoms, Causes, Treatment - How Aerobically Fit Can We Be?" *MedicineNet*, accessed July 26, 2013, http://www.medicinenet.com/aerobic_exercise/article.htm.

8   2 Samuel 6:14 (NLT)

9   2 Samuel 6:16 (NIV): As the ark of the Lord was entering the City of David, Michal daughter of Saul watched from a window. And when she saw King David leaping and dancing before the Lord, she despised him in her heart.

human heart.[10] Therefore, if the eternal is part of the human heart, then we are eternal beings. Our heart talk will connect the eternal within ourselves to the eternal that transcends our existence. In prayer we can communicate with the eternal God, because of the eternal presence of his Son, Jesus Christ, whom we have made Lord of our hearts.[11]

In the prayer exercises in the second half of the book you will have the opportunity through your heart talk to:

- Pour out the contents of your heart, like Hannah, to God. You will practice bringing your worries, anxieties, fears and rejoicing to God;

- Let your heart be searched by God's Holy Spirit and illuminated with God's light;

- Allow your heart to be massaged by God's Spirit to remove hard knots of sin such as jealousy, bitterness, anger, gossip—attributes that make your heart hard;

- Permit your heart to be healed from pain, anger and disappointment;

- Enable your heart to be cleansed and flow with love, joy, peace, gentleness and other fruits of the Spirit.

---

10 Ecclesiastes 3:11 (NIV): He has made everything beautiful in its time. He has also set eternity in the human heart; yet no one can fathom what God has done from beginning to end.

11 1 Peter 3:15 (NIV): But in your hearts revere Christ as Lord.

IN THE ZONE

Use the prayer exercises on the following pages to practice you heart talk:

Prayer Zone Workout 1 will encourage you to speak *openly* and *freely* from your heart with God about everything in your life..

Prayer Zone Workout 2 will teach you to use breath prayer so you can *listen* more attentively to what God wants to say to your heart.

Prayer Zone Workout 3 is to *strengthen* your heart so you will have greater faith and confidence when you pray.

Prayer Zone Workout 4 allows you to *pour out* your heart's anxieties to God.

Prayer Zone Workout 5 encourages you if your thoughts wander during prayer. These thoughts could reveal areas of hardness in your heart. Therefore, this workout will help you *discover* where your heart needs to receive a massage from God to make it softer and purer.

Prayer Zone Workout 6 is an exercise for when you want to *confess* and *receive cleansing* of the heart that God gives.

Prayer Zone Workout 7 is an opportunity for you to bring your pain and anger to God so your heart receives *healing*.

Prayer Zone Workout 8 guides you to pray about temptations and how to *protect* your heart from attack by our spiritual enemy.

Prayer Zone Workout 9 is for when your heart is *thankful* and Prayer Zone Workout 10 is for a heart that is *peaceful*.

The heart is the hub of prayer

Chapter 6
Prayer Zone Workout Structure

Therefore, since we are surrounded by such a great cloud of witnesses, let us throw off everything that hinders and the sin that so easily entangles. And let us run with perseverance the race marked out for us. Hebrews 12:1 (NIV)

So far, you have been learning about my experience with prayer and exercise. Now it is your turn to participate in creating your own Prayer Zone Workout. Soon you'll be experiencing a more satisfying prayer life as you grow healthier in both body and spirit. This chapter guides you through how to do this.

A Prayer Zone Workout is structured much like an aerobic exercise routine: both have a warm-up, a period of high-intensity exercise, a time of low-intensity activity, and then a cool-down.

Flexibility/Preparing for Prayer. Physical exercise begins with a warm-up that involves flexibility exercises. Flexibility exercises are important in any workout routine because they allow you to move more easily and with less risk of injury.

When starting any Prayer Zone Workout, spiritual flexing is just as important. It enables you to pray more easily, and allows you to pray in different ways under different circumstances. Just as you prepare your body for physical activity, you also want to make your heart ready for prayer.

Warm-up/Entering God's Throne Room. Your physical warm-up should involve exercising at a slower pace with lower intensity. It helps prepare the body for more strenuous aerobic and cardiovascular activity later on. Similarly, Entering God's Throne Room is prayer that stirs and awakens our hearts. The prayer warm-up enables your mind and heart to center on being in the presence of God. It helps equip your spiritual heart for the more intense prayer activity that will follow. This phase of the Prayer

Zone Workout corresponds to "Our Father in heaven" in the Lord's Prayer. When Jesus's disciples asked him how to pray, he told them to begin with these words: "Our Father, who art in heaven." When we enter God's Throne Room, we are entering into an intimate encounter with the God who calls us into a personal relationship with him.

High-intensity/Talking to Your Heavenly Father. High-intensity exercise is the most vigorous part of your physical workout, when your body works harder and your heart rate increases. For example, walking uphill or at a quicker pace is considered high-intensity exercise. Likewise, Talking to Your Heavenly Father is a more demanding phase of your prayer work-out. Talking about your worries and struggles, while making requests of God, involves high-intensity prayer. This type of prayer can be passionate, even strenuous. It raises your spiritual heart rate. This phase corresponds to "Give us today our daily bread" in The Lord's Prayer where we ask God for what we need.

Low-intensity/Listening to Your Heavenly Father. Low-intensity exercise is physically less demanding. It enables your body to recover from high-intensity exercise. In the same way, listening to God allows you to take a rest from talking about the worries and concerns of life. Listening enables you to hear what your heavenly Father has to say about the condition of your heart and to see other people from God's perspective. Listening permits the Holy Spirit to do his work of searching and rejuvenating your heart. It is in this phase that you may want to ask God for forgiveness. This coincides with "forgive us our debts, as we also have forgiven our debtors" in The Lord's Prayer.

You can alternate between high-intensity and low-intensity exercise as many times as you want. This, then, becomes your interval training. For your spiritual heart, this interval training is like a conversation. You talk to God, then pause and spend time listening to him before speaking again.

Cool-down/Leaving God's Throne Room. A cool-down is milder form of physical exercise that allows your heart rate to gradually return to normal.

Leaving God's Throne Room is prayer that prepares your mind and spiritual heart for returning to everyday activities. During this phase, you will ask God for peace and protection. This reflects the ending of The Lord's Prayer: "And lead us not into temptation, but deliver us from the evil one."

Although cool-down marks the end of your Prayer Zone Workout, I recommend post-workout stretching to reduce muscle soreness and decrease the chance of injury.

Each Prayer Zone Workout includes all five phases. They are outlined in the table below:

Prayer Zone Workout Routines

Physical Exercise	Spiritual Exercise	Duration
Stretching and Flexibility	Preparing for prayer	5 minutes
Warm-up	Entering God's Throne Room	5 minutes
*High-intensity	Talking to Your Heavenly Father	5 minutes
*Low-intensity	Listening to Your Heavenly Father	10-15 minutes
Cool-down	Leaving God's Throne Room	5 minutes

* Interval training.

Prayer Exercises

The second half of the book features ten prayer exercises. Each prayer exercise is specifically designed to help you care for the health of your spiritual heart. They include the following features:

Length of time for each phase of the prayer exercise. Five minutes is the suggested length of time for each phase, except for Listening to Your Heavenly Father, which requires ten to fifteen minutes. An optimum time for a complete Prayer Zone Workout is thirty to thirty-five minutes. (See the table on the previous page.) However, if thirty-five minutes of exercise and prayer seems overwhelming, then make your Prayer Zone Workout shorter and build up to the thirty-five minutes. Simply break up your workout into shorter segments. To help you get started, you will find that the first complete prayer exercises are only twenty minutes long.

Words from scripture. Each verse taken from the Bible relates to one phase of the prayer exercises. It is designed to help you focus and ensure your prayer is grounded in God's word. I draw my scripture references from several translations of the Bible. A list of abbreviations with "Bible translations" can be found in the appendix.

Meditation guidance. This provides direction on how to pray during a particular exercise. It also guides you in the use of breathing exercises, your spiritual imagination, your mind, and your heart as you pray.

Journal. Journal entries from my own Prayer Zone Workouts are included with each prayer exercise. These are meant to inspire and motivate you to incorporate prayer into your daily routine. Consider starting your own Prayer Zone Workout journal. After completing your daily Prayer Zone Workout, spend a few minutes writing down the highlights of your heart talk. This can help you clarify and experience more deeply what was spoken and discerned. Journaling offers many other benefits. Over time, you may want to revisit your journals to see how God is changing and molding your heart and life to make you fitter and healthier. Interestingly, journaling has also been found to improve physical and mental health,[1] so together with your healthier physical and spiritual heart, your whole life can benefit.

IN THE ZONE

Spend a few minutes familiarizing yourself with the structure of the Prayer Zone Workout. Look through the Prayer Zone Workout exercises provided in the following chapters. You can also find these exercises on the Prayer Zone Workout website: www.prayerzoneworkout.com. Here you can print out exercises in a handy size and format to take with you during your Prayer Zone Workout.

Or download the Prayer Zone Workout application for your smartphone, which enables you to use the exercises from your smartphone or tablet. (More information is available in the appendix.)

Before your first Prayer Zone Workout, commit to a start date. Look back at your Prayer Zone Workout Plan at the end of Chapter Three. Make sure you are prepared for your chosen physical exercise. Do you have good sneakers for walking or running? Is your bicycle in good working condition? Have you put together a Prayer Zone Workout group and organized your first meeting?

Now look forward to and begin with Prayer Zone Workout Day 1 on the following page. Remember, this is the start to a fitter and healthier body and soul. Use the verse at the beginning of the chapter to encourage you: *Therefore, since we are surrounded by such a great cloud of witnesses, let us throw off everything that hinders and the sin that so easily entangles. And let us run with perseverance the race marked out for us.* Hebrews 12:1 (NIV)

Practice prayer with perseverance.

---

1   "Writing and Health," accessed September 13, 2013, http://homepage.psy.utexas.edu/ homepage/faculty/pennebaker/home2000/WritingandHealth.html

The Workouts

Prayer Zone Workout 1

During Prayer Zone Workout 1 you will be using the prayer exercise below with your chosen physical exercise.

The first prayer exercise is designed to help you focus on spending time with God. This workout is intended to help you linger in conversation with your heavenly Father and for you to sense the pleasure he experiences when you pray to him.

This exercise will give you an opportunity to pray for twenty minutes while completing a twenty-minute physical workout. Read through and contemplate the guidance given in the prayer exercise and then follow the IN THE ZONE instructions.

Preparing for Prayer: In this workout you will

- Begin by praying to God who is in heaven, yet who is also present with you in all places and at all times;

- Practice talking about all things in your life with God, who sees everything, and perceives all your desires and thoughts;

- Practice listening to God with the help of the Holy Spirit;

- And finish today's workout by making a commitment to pray and exercise regularly.

Entering God's Throne Room

Coming to God's Throne. God, the sovereign ruler of the universe, longs for you to come into his presence and spend time with him.

Our Lord and our God, I turn my eyes to you on your throne in heaven. Psalm 123:1 (CEV)

Meditation guidance

- **Imagine** coming into the presence of God in his throne room. Use this image of God from scripture to help you:

You are dressed in a robe of light. You stretch out the starry curtain of the heavens; you lay out the rafters of your home in the rain clouds. You make the clouds your chariot; you ride upon the wings of the wind. Psalm 104:2-3 (NLT)

- **Meditate on** how one scripture writer describes God—for no one has seen God because God is Spirit.

The one sitting on the throne was as brilliant as gemstones—like jasper and carnelian. And the glow of an emerald circled his throne like a rainbow. Revelation 4:3 (NLT)

- **Reflect on** God's splendor and grandeur, and his power and authority.

God is King, robed and ruling, God is robed and surging with strength. And yes, the world is firm, immovable, your throne ever firm—you're Eternal! Psalm 93:1 (MSG)

Talking to your heavenly Father

Talking about everything. Talk to your heavenly Father about everything that is on your mind and heart. God knows you intimately—the details of your life, the thoughts of your mind, and the feelings of your heart. You can be honest and open with him.

The Lord sees everything you do. Wherever you go, he is watching. Proverbs 5:21 (GNT)

Meditation guidance:

- **Talk to** your heavenly Father about the things that are going on in your life: your plans, troubles, joys, and fears.

  Pray in the Spirit on all occasions with all kinds of prayers and requests. Ephesians 6:18 (NIV)

- **Speak** openly and honestly to your heavenly Father. You are no stranger to God. He knows even the deepest secrets of your heart.

  You have looked deep into my heart, Lord, and you know all about me. You know when I am resting or when I am working, and from heaven you discover my thoughts. You notice everything I do and everywhere I go. Before I even speak a word, you know what I will say. Psalm 139:1-4 (CEV)

- **Express** your commitment to prayer; to talk intimately with your heavenly Father on a regular basis.

  Devote yourselves to prayer. Colossians 4:2 (NLT)

Listening to your heavenly Father

Breathing in the Holy Spirit. God sent his Holy Spirit to be your helper. The Holy Spirit will guide your listening and your response.

But the Holy Spirit will come and help you, because the Father will send the Spirit to take my place. John 14:26 (CEV)

Meditation guidance

- **Take notice** of your breathing. Take deep breaths. With each intake of air, imagine the Holy Spirit coming into your heart and him teaching you how to listen to God.

The Spirit will teach you everything and will remind you of what I said while I was with you. John 14:26 (CEV)

- **Be attentive** to the Holy Spirit dwelling within you.

You surely know that your body is a temple where the Holy Spirit lives. The Spirit is in you and is a gift from God. 1 Corinthians 6:19 (CEV)

- **Concentrate on** receiving the Holy Spirit.

Then he took a deep breath and breathed into them. "Receive the Holy Spirit," he said. John 20:22 (MSG)

Leaving God's throne room

A healthy heart. As you leave this time spent with God in his throne room, reflect on how you have exercised your spiritual heart along with your physical body during your Prayer Zone Workout.

Physical training is good, but training for godliness is much better, promising benefits in this life and in the life to come. 1 Timothy 4:8 (NLT)

Meditation guidance

- **Reflect on** how the time spent with God while you exercise makes your body physically fitter and your heart spiritually healthier. What benefits can this focused attention to prayer and exercise bring to your mind, body and soul during this workout?

- **Meditate on** what you hear, if anything, from God during this time, and during the rest of your day.

  Trust God from the bottom of your heart; don't try to figure out everything on your own. Listen for God's voice in everything you do, everywhere you go; he's the one who will keep you on track. Proverbs 3:5-6 (MSG)

- **Ask** your heavenly Father to help you live a revitalized and healthy life.

IN THE ZONE

God is always present with you, your constant companion. Your Prayer Zone Workout is your special time, in your sacred place, to spend time with God. Make a plan to complete this workout during the next few days.

Make a list of the things you want to pray about—events, plans and desires, fears and troubles, needs and wants, struggles and temptations, comforts and pleasures. These will be more than enough to fill five minutes of prayer.

Commit to having a regular and consistent Prayer Zone Workout so you have the opportunity to talk to God about everything in your life.

God knows you better than your best friend, your spouse, even better than you know yourself. Do you feel comfortable talking to God, even about those things hidden in your heart that you would not share with anyone else? Or are your prayers usually like a polite conversation with a stranger? Do you compartmentalize your thoughts—bringing respectable aspects of your life to your prayers, but keeping unrespectable things to yourself?

The suggested time for each phase of this workout is five minutes. This will give you a twenty-minute workout. You can make a longer workout by adding an extra five or ten minutes to the listening segment of the workout.

Look back at the prayer exercise. Are there any thoughts expressed or scripture verses that you would like to bring with you to your Prayer Zone Workout? Make a note, or jot down a verse, and carry it with you for reference during your workout. Alternatively, print out prayer exercises in a condensed format from the Prayer Zone Workout website—www.prayer-zoneworkout.com, or download the Prayer Zone Workout app (see Appendix 1), which enables you to use the exercises from your smartphone.

Read my own experience of learning to spend time with God in the Prayer Zone Journal Day 1 entry.

Prayer Zone Journal: Day 1

Lingering in the Doorway

June 7 – Day 1: Practice of Prayer course

I am to imagine coming into God's throne room to pray to him. This should be easy for a British person like myself, raised with the rich history of kings and queens, castles and palaces, thrones and throne rooms. However, this does not prepare me for the heavenly Father's throne room.

I stand at the entrance between immense and imposing marble pillars that seem to reach into eternity. I hesitate. Confidence eludes me. I cannot place my foot over the threshold. A huge room stretches before me; bounded by clouds and a deep blue the sky. Crowds of people—the witnesses whom I have read about in Hebrews—congregate in God's throne room. I sense their cheerfulness. Still, I am not persuaded. For some reason, I find it difficult coming before God.

Thoughts flood my mind. How have I prayed to God prior to this occasion? Had I really thought about God? Did I only launch prayers into outer space—in God's general direction—and addressed to him, expecting him to pick them up? Until now, I considered my praying a job well done. I mean, I had been praying! I would fire off a silent prayer when the thought entered my mind. Or I might pray out loud when on my own.

Now, however, I understand my prayers have been merely vague thoughts stuffed in an envelope with "God" scrawled on the outside. This doesn't make them personal prayers.

I am more than a little rusty with prayer. I have never practiced talking intimately to God. Shame keeps me on the threshold. I hang my head, look at the floor and shuffle my feet.

Yet I know God wants me to be with him. God sacrificed his Son for this purpose. God's inner sanctum wasn't always accessible to ordinary people, but Jesus made it possible for anyone to come into God's presence. Jesus' death opened the doorway to heaven.

I have lingered enough. I am able to walk beyond the marble pillars. So, I step over the threshold.

Journal Reflection

How do you perceive God when you pray to him? What emotions do you experience? What have you heard, read, seen, or experienced that influences your concept of God?

Do you experience any difficulties walking over the threshold into God's presence? Do you know his throne room as a place where you belong?

Bring your thoughts on these questions to God during your Prayer Zone Workout. Then, from your prayer experience, write your own Prayer Zone Journal entry.

Prayer is making all your thoughts into talk.

Prayer Zone Workout 2

During Prayer Zone Workout 2 you will be using the prayer exercise below with your chosen physical exercise.

This prayer exercise is to help you practice bringing your daily needs to God as your heavenly Father. Often, we have difficulty conceiving of God as a loving and caring Father. Therefore, this workout is an opportunity for you to work through any barriers to having a healthy relationship with God.

This prayer exercise will give you an opportunity to pray and exercise for twenty minutes within a twenty-minute physical workout. Read through and contemplate the guidance given in the prayer exercise and then follow the IN THE ZONE instructions.

Preparing for Prayer: In this workout you will

- Begin by praying to God as your Father in heaven, using The Lord's Prayer as your model;

- Practice asking your heavenly Father for the things you need. This is also called making personal petitions;

- Practice "breath prayer" and use this method of praying to listen to God. This ancient practice of prayer originated in the Eastern Christian tradition. It uses a short phrase that is repeated silently with each breath. The most well-known breath prayer is called the Jesus Prayer, which uses the phrase "Lord Jesus Christ, Son of God, have mercy on me, a sinner;" and

- Finish today's workout remembering God promises to be with you and meet all your needs.

Entering God's Throne Room

God, your heavenly Father. Jesus taught us to pray to God as our Father in heaven. God wants you to know him as your divine Father. Come into God's throne room and call him Abba or Papa.

You should pray like this: "Our Father in heaven..." Matthew 6:9 *(CEV)*

Meditation guidance
- **Imagine** coming into God's majestic throne room. Call out the name of your heavenly Father: *Abba,* or even *Papa.* Repeat his name as you come into his presence.

- **Meditate on** God, your heavenly Father, who delights to have you, his child, present with him. Use this scripture to help you:

  I have always wanted to treat you as my children...I wanted you to call me "Father" and not turn from me. Jeremiah 3:19 (CEV)

- **Reflect on** your heavenly Father, who is always waiting to hear from you. He is ready and eager to respond when you turn to him. God, your Father, says:

  I've made myself available to those who haven't bothered to ask. I'm here, ready to be found by those who haven't bothered to look. I kept saying, "I'm here, I'm right here." Isaiah 65:1-2 (MSG)

Talking to your heavenly Father

Coming with requests. Your heavenly Father wants you to ask him for what you need. God is willing and eager to respond. Bring your needs to him and trust him with the answers.

Don't worry about anything; instead pray about everything. Tell God what you need, and thank him for all he has done. Philippians 4:6 (NLT)

Meditation guidance

- **Talk to** God, your Father, about your needs even though

  Your Father knows what you need before you ask. Matthew 6:8 (NIV)

- **Speak to** your heavenly Father about how he meets your needs.

  And with all his abundant wealth through Christ Jesus, my God will supply all your needs. Philippians 4:19 (GNT)

- **Express** your trust in God to meet your requests. Remember God promises to provide everything you need for life. Use these words:

  Some trust in chariots and some in horses, but we trust in the name of the Lord our God. Psalm 20:7 (NIV)

Listening to your heavenly Father

Breathing in the Holy Spirit. Concentrate on your breathing and practice breath prayer using the phrase from 1 Samuel 3:10 below.

But it is the spirit in a person, the breath of the Almighty, that gives them understanding. Job 32:8 (NIV)

Meditation guidance

- **Take notice** of any areas of tension in your body. Relax your shoulders. Hold your hands palm up.

- **Be attentive** to your breath. Breathe naturally. Repeat the words from this scriptures with each breath: As you breathe in say:

  Speak, and as you breathe out say: Your servant is listening. 1 Samuel 3:10 (NLT)

- **Concentrate on** your words. If your mind wanders, redirect it to the phrase. Listen to God's response:

  Even before they finish praying to me, I will answer their prayers. Isaiah 65:24 (GNT)

Leaving God's throne room

You heavenly Father protects you. God will always keep you safe. As you leave God's throne room, focus on your heavenly Father's promise of safe-keeping.

Whoever trusts in the Lord is kept safe. Proverbs 29:25 (NIV)

Meditation guidance

- **Reflect on** the answer to these questions about God, who gives you protection:

  Won't God protect his chosen ones who pray to him day and night? Won't he be concerned for them? He will surely hurry and help them. Luke 18:7-8 (CEV)

- **Meditate on** these words as you prepare to leave the security of your heavenly Father's throne room:

  But blessed are those who trust in the Lord and have made the Lord their hope and confidence. They are like trees planted along a riverbank, with roots that reach deep into the water. Such trees are not bothered by the heat or worried by long months of drought. Their leaves stay green, and they never stop producing fruit. Jeremiah 17:7-8 (NLT)

- **Tell** your heavenly Father that you trust him for the protection that you need as you go into your daily life. Repeat the words of this scripture:

  You are my place of safety and my shield. Psalm 119:114 (CEV)

IN THE ZONE

God longs for you to pray to him as your heavenly Father. Start your Prayer Zone workout by beginning with the word Abba, Papa or Father.

What do you need to ask your heavenly Father for today? Make a list of your immediate concerns and needs—the "daily" bread, as in The Lord's Prayer. Bring these requests to your workout.

Many religions and practices use the technique of mindful breathing to aid relaxation When this technique is practiced with Christian prayer, it helps you release stress to your heavenly Father instead of merely escaping it.[1] Commit to making breath prayer a regular part of your praying.

You will find a Prayer Zone Workout breath prayer video on the Prayer Zone Workout website: www.prayerzoneworkout.com that guides you through this practice.

Read my experience of praying to God as my Father in the Prayer Zone Journal Day 2.

---

1   "Breath Prayer: Sophrony's Longing for Communion," n.d., http://tenwaystopray.com/home/breath-sophrony/.

Prayer Zone Journal: Day 2

Daddy

June 7 – Practice of Prayer Course

Today, I come to the vast marble pillars of God's throne room to pray to God as *Abba*—to talk to the divine as my heavenly "Daddy." I am uncomfortable being this intimate with God. I unearth a question from the bottom of my heart: *Don't you, of unsurpassed greatness, require me to be polite and dutiful, like a Victorian child?*

Again, I hesitate on the threshold, pondering the paradox of a formidable God who is also a tender Father. Yet to understand it, I must practice repeating God's name: *Abba, Abba, Abba, Abba.*

At first my cries of *Abba* are like a timid toddler when her parent is on the other side of the room. I take tentative steps into God's glorious throne room and speak the word *Abba*. I sense this mighty, powerful God encouraging my first steps. He longs for me to come close and call him *Abba*. I hear my heavenly Father call me *daughter*. I *am* his daughter.

My heart beats faster and my eyes fill with tears. I feel the warmth of Abba's love for me. I totter, but my stumbling steps become more assured the closer I get, like the toddler before she falls into the arms of her parent. I no longer cling to the marble pillars of God's throne room. Instead, I have confidently entered the splendid place where I can spend precious time with my heavenly "Daddy."

Journal Reflection
What is your perception of God as your heavenly Father?

What stumbling blocks keep you from praying freely to God as your Father? Does your relationship with your own earthly father affect your understanding of God as your Father?

How does the knowledge and tension of a human being in relationship with his or her divine Father affect your prayers?

What thoughts and emotions do you experience when you come to God the perfect Father even though you are not yet a perfect child? Are you overawed? Do you understand his compassionate love for you?

Use this prayer exercise with the truths of scripture, and the help of the Holy Spirit to work out any wrongly perceived ideas you have of your heavenly Father and to help you gain a true understanding of God as your Father.

Prayer is letting the heavenly Father lavish you with love.

Prayer Zone Workout 3

During Prayer Zone Workout 3 you will be using the prayer exercise below with your chosen physical exercise.

This prayer exercise is to help you make requests and petitions with faith and confidence. Sometimes, asking God to give you the desires of your heart is difficult. You may doubt that God will grant your request, and sometimes he does not. Therefore, this exercise aims to build your faith and confidence in God rather than focusing on your requests.

This exercise will give you an opportunity to pray for twenty minutes while completing a twenty-minute physical workout. Read through and contemplate the guidance given in the prayer exercise and then follow the IN THE ZONE instructions.

Preparing for Prayer: In this workout you will

- Begin by praying to God as the creator of the world;

- Practice asking God, with faith and confidence, for what you need—believing that God is sufficient to meet those needs and that you will receive good things from God.

- Practice listening to God using breath prayer; and

- Finish today's workout by considering how God can provide you with wisdom and understanding to live a contented life.

Entering God's Throne Room

God, your creator. The world is God's creation. Come into the presence of God, the creator. God created the world; and he created you, too.

In the beginning you laid the foundations of the earth, and the heavens are the work of your hands. Psalm 102:25 (NIV)

Meditation guidance

- **Imagine** God creating the world, the world that is around you. Consider this scripture:

He made the earth by his power; he founded the world by his wisdom and stretched out the heavens by his understanding. Jeremiah 51:15 (NIV)

- **Meditate on** God's creation of *you*. Use this scripture to help you:

You created every part of me; you put me together in my mother's womb. Psalm 139:13 (GNT)

- **Reflect on** and worship God, your creator.

God is the best, High King over all the gods. In one hand he holds deep caves and caverns, in the other hand he grasps the high mountains. He made Ocean—he owns it! His hands sculpted Earth! So come, let us worship: bow before him, on your knees before God, who made us! Psalm 95:3-6 (MSG)

Talking to your heavenly Father

Asking with faith and confidence. Bring your requests to God. Ask with faith and confidence, knowing that your heavenly Father has your best interests at heart.

"For I know the plans I have for you," declares the Lord, "plans to prosper you and not to harm you, plans to give you hope and a future." Jeremiah 29:11(NIV)

Meditation guidance

- **Talk to** your heavenly Father about the confidence you have in him to give you good things.

Would any of you who are fathers give your son a stone when he asks for bread? Or would you give him a snake when he asks for a fish? As bad as you are, you know how to give good things to your children. How much more, then, will your Father in heaven give good things to those who ask him! Matthew 7:9-11 (GNT)

- **Speak to** God about your faith in him.

If you remain in me and my words remain in you, ask whatever you wish, and it will be done for you. John 15:7 (NIV)

- **Express** your requests with confidence and faith in God.

Ask boldly, believingly, without a second thought. James 1:6 (MSG)

Listening to your heavenly Father

Breathing in the Holy Spirit. Concentrate on your breathing and practice breath prayer using the phrase from Mark 9:24 below.

But it is the spirit in a person, the breath of the Almighty, that gives them understanding. Job 32:8 (NIV)

Meditation guidance

- **Take notice** of any areas of tension in your body. Relax your shoulders. Hold your hands palm up.

- **Be attentive** to your breath. Breathe naturally. Repeat the words from this scripture with each breath.

  As you breathe in say: "I do have faith." As you breathe out say: "help me to have more!" Mark 9:24 (TLB)

- **Concentrate on** your words. If your mind wanders, redirect it to the phrase. Then listen to Jesus' words:

  "Your faith has saved you; go in peace." Luke 7:50 (NIV)

Leaving God's Throne Room

Living a life of contentment. As you leave God's throne room, reflect on how you should live with faith and confidence.

So be careful how you live. Don't live like fools, but like those who are wise. Ephesians 5:15 (NLT)

Meditation guidance

- **Reflect on** the requests you made earlier. Would you change any of these requests?

God planned for us to do good things and to live as he has always wanted us to live. Ephesians 2:10 (CEV)

- **Meditate on** God's generosity to provide you with wisdom and understanding

If any of you lacks wisdom, you should ask God, who gives generously to all without finding fault, and it will be given to you. But when you ask, you must believe and not doubt. James 1:5-6 (NIV)

- **Tell** God that you want to live a satisfying life. Ask him to renew you from the inside out.

And then take on an entirely new way of life—a God-fashioned life, a life renewed from the inside and working itself into your conduct as God accurately reproduces his character in you. Ephesians 4:24 (MSG)

IN THE ZONE

How does knowing God as creator help you have faith and confidence in him?

What requests do you need to make with faith and confidence in God? Do you find your faith and confidence in God is based on how he answers your request? Does your faith waver if God does not grant your request? Do you lose confidence in God's promise to give you good things and a hope and a future if your requests are not answered in the way you want?

Use the practice of breath prayer to help you listen to God and to reflect on your requests and the answers God gives.

Read my experience of praying with faith and confidence in the Prayer Zone Journal Day 3.

Prayer Zone Journal: Day 3

Having confidence in unanswered prayers
November 2 - Duration: 42:00 minutes - Start time: 11:41 a.m. - End time: 12:30
p.m. - Pace: 16:12/mile - Distance: 2.12 miles - Calories: 168

Sometimes my requests made to God are not answered in the way I want. Then I feel like a child who only gets to look through the window of a candy store. I'm not sure children usually questions their parent's loving care in this kind of situation, but I often dispute God's love for me and see his answers as rejection. Then I chew over whether I have asked with a lack of faith or with the wrong motives, that my requests are selfish, or outside God's plans. I tie myself in knots in this way.

Today's petition is a request I have made repeatedly for sixteen years. I'm still waiting for it to be answered in a way that meets with my heart's desires.

I would like to move away from here. Please make it happen. I don't want to live here anymore. I never really wanted to live here. I think I would be happier if we moved. There is nothing wrong with where we live. But for me, it is not home. I am a native of England, not New England. Moving back home seems appealing on the surface, but underneath I'm not completely sure. I like some aspects of living here. I don't specifically admit this to God, instead I add: *Living somewhere else in the world would be better. Anywhere but here.*

People around me come and go. Our town is full of people relocating to and from other parts of the world, but our location has not changed in sixteen years. *I never imagined living here for so long.* We are firmly stuck, as if in mud. Circumstances do not allow us to leave New England.

Your plans for me must be different from my own, I acknowledge reluctantly staring at the track as I walk. Scripture says they are better, but I only consider God stalling on my request. *If you want me to stay here, then you have to provide me with strength to do so.* Yet, my heart is not in these words. I ask for strength, but I would rather not have it.

My thoughts turn to the story of Joseph. He, too, lived away from his homeland, and struggled to come to terms with his circumstances. He shed many tears. Yet, he remained faithful to God. Eventually, Joseph understood God's plan for his life.

I consider my own meager faithfulness, and how disgruntled I get with God. *I too, need to remain faithful to you. Help me to see that you have a good plan. Give me wisdom and understanding.*

Suddenly, out of the corner of my eye I spot pink sweatpants and a pink knitted hat worn by a person running slowly on the inside lane. The Pink Apparition passes surprisingly close. No longer "stuck in Egypt," I watch as she jogs around the bend and down the straight. Then as quickly as she appeared, she is gone—into the parking lot and climbs into a rather nondescript minivan.

Journal Reflection

If your requests are not being answered in the way you want, do you find it difficult to accept God's answer? What is your reaction towards God? Are you being completely honest with God about your feelings towards him with regard to your "unanswered" prayer?

Bring your struggles and disappointments with unanswered prayer to God and *work* them *out* with him. Ask him to give you peace and understanding about the answers to your prayers.

During this Prayer Zone Workout, bring one specific, but difficult, request to God and ask him for wisdom and understanding. Perhaps it is a request that you have made on numerous occasions. Write about your prayer experience in a Prayer Zone Journal entry. Repeat this prayer exercise as many times as necessary, until you feel at peace. Then look back at your original journal entry to see how God has given you understanding about your request.

Prayer is having faith in a faithful God.

Prayer Zone Workout 4

During Prayer Zone Workout 4 you will be using the prayer exercise below with your chosen physical exercise.

Use this prayer exercise to help ease stress when you are anxious. Tension in the physical body can be relieved through physical exercise, and prayer can help you manage stress. Scripture promises that your anxieties will be replaced by God's peace when you pray. Engaging in this prayer exercise will improve your overall sense of well-being.

This prayer exercise will give you an opportunity to pray for twenty minutes while completing a twenty-minute physical workout. Read through and contemplate the guidance given in the prayer exercise and then follow the IN THE ZONE instructions.

Preparing for Prayer: In this workout you will

- Begin by praying to God, who is holy and pure; remember God is your Father and he cares for you;

- Practice bringing your anxieties to God. Scripture teaches that this will ease your fears, you will receive peace from God, and your heart and mind will be protected;

- Practice breath prayer to reduce tension in your mind and body. This will help you experience the inside-out peace that comes from God through the presence of his Spirit; and

- Finish today's workout reflecting on the promises of God as armor and protection.

Entering God's Throne Room

A holy and pure God. God is perfect, holy, and pure. God is set apart from you in his holiness, yet you are welcome and accepted in his presence.

There is no one holy like the Lord. 1 Samuel 2:2 (NIV)

Meditation guidance.

- **Imagine** standing, kneeling, or lying prostrate before God. Worship God in his holiness, yet know this does not make him distant or unapproachable.

Exalt the Lord our God and worship at his footstool; he is holy. Psalm 99:5 (NIV)

- **Meditate on** Jesus Christ who enables you to have full access to a holy God and who taught us to pray in this way:

Hallowed be your name. Luke 11:2 (NIV)

So, friends, we can now—without hesitation—walk right up to God, into "the Holy Place." Jesus has cleared the way by the blood of his sacrifice, acting as our priest before God. The "curtain" into God's presence is his body. So let's do it—full of belief, confident that we're presentable inside and out. Hebrews 10:19-22 (MSG)

- **Reflect on** knowing that God, the holy one, also lives within you.

A message from the high and towering God, who lives in Eternity, whose name is Holy: "I live in the high and holy places, but also with the low-spirited, the spirit-crushed, and what I do is put new spirit in them, get them up and on their feet again." Isaiah 57:15 (MSG)

Talking to your heavenly Father

Bringing your anxieties to God. In God's throne room, talk to your heavenly Father about the troubles in your life—your worries, hurts, and fears. Remember that your heavenly Father hears your cries.

As for me, I call to God, and the Lord saves me. Evening, morning and noon I cry out in distress, and he hears my voice. Psalm 55:16-17 (NIV)

Meditation guidance.
- **Talk to** God, your Father, about what is worrying you.

  Do not be anxious about anything, but in every situation, by prayer and petition, with thanksgiving, present your requests to God. Philippians 4:6 (NIV)

- **Speak to** your Father about your troubles. Remember he is always with you.

  I will never leave you; I will never abandon you. Hebrews 13:5 (GNT)

- **Express** your response to these words spoken to you by your heavenly Father:

  Do not be anxious about anything, but in every situation, by prayer and petition, with thanksgiving, present your requests to God. And the peace of God, which transcends all understanding, will guard your hearts and your minds in Christ Jesus. Philippians 4:6-7 (NIV)

Listening to your heavenly Father

Breathing in the Holy Spirit. God sent his Holy Spirit to be your helper. The Holy Spirit will bring relief from your anxieties.

But the Holy Spirit will come and help you, because the Father will send the Spirit to take my place. John 14:26 (CEV)

Meditation guidance
- **Take notice** of your breathing. Take deep breaths. With each intake of air, imagine breathing the Holy Spirit into your heart, and him bringing you God's peace.

You, LORD, give perfect peace to those who keep their purpose firm and put their trust in you. Isaiah 26:3 (GNT)

- **Be attentive** to the Holy Spirit within you.

You surely know that your body is a temple where the Holy Spirit lives. The Spirit is in you and is a gift from God. 1 Corinthians 6:19 (CEV)

- **Concentrate on** receiving the Holy Spirit.

Then he took a deep breath and breathed into them. "Receive the Holy Spirit," he said. John 20:22 (MSG)

Leaving God's Throne Room

Putting on God's armor. As you leave your heavenly Father's throne room and go out to face your day, focus on the armor of God that protects you.

He will cover you with his feathers. He will shelter you with his wings. His faithful promises are your armor and protection. Psalm 91:4 (NLT)

Meditation guidance

- **Reflect on** the promises of God:

"I will rescue those who love me. I will protect those who trust in my name. When they call on me, I will answer; I will be with them in trouble. I will rescue and honor them." Psalm 91:14-15 (NLT)

- **Meditate on** these words:

If you are tired from carrying heavy burdens, come to me and I will give you rest. Matthew 11:28 (CEV)

- **Tell** God, as you prepare to leave your Prayer Zone Workout, that you will stay close and trust him, even though your heart may still be heavy with concerns.

The Lord is my strength and my shield; my heart trusts in him, and he helps me. Psalm 28:7 (NIV)

IN THE ZONE

What worries are burdening you today? Practice bringing *all* your anxieties to God. As you pray, imagine filling a sack with your concerns. Bring your worries to God and place them in the sack. Carry the sack to the steps of God's throne and leave it there.

Physical exercise, deep breathing, and prayer have been proven to relieve the physical side effects of stress. You will receive health benefits when you practice these elements in your workout.

How do you understand the life-changing peace that God's gives? Do you understand it as an external change in external circumstances, or an inner peace that takes place regardless of your circumstances?

Commit to talking regularly with your heavenly Father. The more time you spend in prayer, the more turning over your anxieties to God will become automatic, and the more you will experience "the peace of God that surpasses all understanding."

Read my experience of praying when I was anxious in Prayer Zone Journal Day 4.

Prayer Zone Journal Day 4

Anxious is an understatement

January 30 - Duration: 32:45 minutes - Start time: 7:35 a.m. - End time: 8:08 a.m. Pace: 16:55/mile - Distance: 1.94 miles - Calories: 154

It is the middle of winter, and yet the air is sultry. A full and shining sun, rising above the bare trees at the end of the track, warms my body through layers of clothes. The fine weather brings the regulars out of hibernation. The office worker dons a peaked, not woolen, cap. He strides ahead of me, but I pass him on the curve of the track. A woman jogs in her place on the inside loop. I admire how she runs so easily. Then I spy pink boots sparkling in the sunlight: the Pink Apparition! I smile.

However, on this outwardly pleasant day, inwardly, butterflies agitate my stomach and interfere with my appetite.

My feet drag on the track while an impending hospital visit later in the day pervades my mind. —

I'm scared.

Scripture tells us to not worry, and instead, to pray.[1] *This is easier said than done.*

Worry took up residence in my mind and heart two weeks ago, after the initial picture of the offending lump on the mammogram and the following invasive biopsies. I have attempted to pray, but worrying comes easier.

Birds chirp cheerfully in the bushes beside the track. *I am more valuable than they are; so I should not worry.*[2] This thought has difficulty finding its way from my head to my heart.

I breathe in deeply and exhale laboriously. I remember Jesus praying when he was deeply burdened by the task ahead of him, before he was captured and put to death. His anguish poured out in his sweat and fell like drops of blood to the ground.[3] I plod on and lose track of the number of

---

1   Philippians 4:6 (MSG): Don't fret or worry. Instead of worrying, pray.
2   Matthew 6:25-26 (NLT): That is why I tell you not to worry about everyday life... Look at the birds. They don't plant or harvest or store food in barns, for your heavenly Father feeds them. And aren't you far more valuable to him than they are?
3   Luke 22:44 (NIV): And being in anguish, he prayed more earnestly, and his sweat was like drops of blood falling to the ground.

times I circle the track.

Anxious thoughts don't flow as eloquent words. Instead, they freeze in my mind. Occasionally I chip away a bite-size prayer: *I'm frightened. Help me.* My anxiety is not subsiding. Jesus, I realize, experienced the same. When he was deeply distressed and troubled, he returned to prayer three times.[4] It's comforting to know that in his humanness, he experienced the same anxiety and fear as I'm feeling now.

I think about family, friends, and people at my church—even those I don't really know well—who are praying for me. They have surged into action and pour out the prayers I cannot express. I think about Jesus again. He wanted his friends to pray, but they just fell asleep.[5]

Jesus walks with those who suffer. Today, I imagine him with me on the track. We walk in step with each other. He keeps pace with my footfalls. *You understand what I am facing today*, I think. I will meet with three doctors to hear the treatment they are recommending for my recently diagnosed breast cancer.

I loop the track, again.

It's comforting to talk with Jesus: *Please don't let any more bad things happen to me right now. I don't think I could take it. But, if they do, be right there with me. Let me feel your presence.*

"You know how difficult this is," I say to him. *"You've been to hell and back, right? This sure feels like hell."*

I turn the corner of the track, the wind whips my face, and I battle to maintain my pace. *Please give me courage to get through today.*

Jesus prayed when he was deeply distressed, and an angel came to strengthen him.[6] I'm reminded of God's promise in scripture that he will never leave or abandon me.[7] *Let me feel you right beside me, walking with me, into hospital today.*

---

4   Mark 14:32-41
5   Mark 14:32-41
6   Luke 22:43
7   I will never leave you nor forsake you. Joshua 1:5 (NIV)

Journal Reflection

Do you find it difficult to pray when you are anxious or fearful about your circumstances? Do you have other people who can pray for you?

Does focusing on Jesus help you know that he understands your suffering, and that God is with you through this experience?

During your workout, practice remembering the promises of God—that he will protect you and will never leave you. Wear these promises as your spiritual armor. Remember that you are not expected to run a marathon in this armor, it is to help you stand firm despite all your worries and fears.

Prayer is channeling your despair into prayer.

Prayer Zone Workout 5

During Prayer Zone Workout 5 you will be using the prayer exercise below with your chosen physical exercise.

Use this prayer exercise to pray for your family, friends, colleagues, and for any person with whom you have a relationship.

This prayer exercise will give you an opportunity to pray and exercise for twenty-five minutes within a twenty-five minute physical workout. Read through and contemplate the guidance given in the prayer exercise and then follow the IN THE ZONE instructions.

Preparing for Prayer. In this workout you will

- Begin by praying to God who accepts *you* just as you are;

- Practice praying for other people and making requests on their behalf. This is called intercession. Thank God for them and the good things in their lives. Pray about your relationships with and your attitude and behavior towards these people;

- Practice listening and making all thoughts, even those that wander, into prayer; and

- Finish today's workout by asking God for guidance.

Entering God's Throne Room

Receiving God's favor. Come to a God who accepts *you*. He will not turn you away, for Jesus Christ has met all the requirements necessary for you to enter God's throne room. Meditate on God's favor, freely given through the sacrifice of his Son on your behalf.

But I pray to you, Lord, in the time of your favor. Psalm 69:13 (NIV)

Meditation guidance

- **Imagine** coming into God's throne room and into the presence of Jesus Christ. Fix your eyes on Jesus.

  For Christ did not enter into a holy place made with human hands, which was only a copy of the true one in heaven. He entered into heaven itself to appear now before God on our behalf. Hebrews 9:24 (NLT)

- **Meditate on** the work of Jesus Christ who enables you, in your unworthiness, to approach with confidence a holy and awesome God.

  We have peace with God because of what Jesus Christ our Lord has done for us...Christ has brought us into this place of undeserved privilege where we now stand...When we were utterly helpless, Christ came at just the right time and died for us sinners...And since we have been made right in God's sight by the blood of Christ...we can rejoice in our wonderful new relationship with God because our Lord Jesus Christ has made us friends of God. Romans 5:1-11 (NLT)

- **Reflect on** what you feel in your heart about Jesus Christ. Bring what is in your heart to him.

Talking to your heavenly Father

Pleas and petitions for others. In God's throne room, bring appeals and requests on behalf of those people in your life who are in need. Pray to your heavenly Father about your relationship with them and your attitude and behavior towards them.

Pray for all people. Ask God to help them; intercede on their behalf, and give thanks for them. 1 Timothy 2:1 (NLT)

Meditation guidance

- **Talk to** God about these people—their anxieties and concerns. Make requests on their behalf. Picture bringing them to Jesus. Remember how, in scripture, needy people were brought before Jesus, who granted their requests.

  Some men brought to him a paralyzed man, lying on a mat. When Jesus saw their faith, he said to the man, "Take heart, son; your sins are forgiven." Matthew 9:2 (NIV)

- **Speak to** your heavenly Father about your relationship, attitude and behavior, particularly areas of difficulty with the people for whom you have just prayed.

- **Express** thanks to God for each person and for the good things in his or her life.

  I have not stopped giving thanks for you, remembering you in my prayers. Ephesians 1:16 (NIV)

Listening to your heavenly Father

Breath prayer. Practice breath prayer using Psalm 139:23 below and allow God's Spirit to search and examine your heart.

But it is the spirit in a person, the breath of the Almighty, that gives them understanding. Job 32:8 (NIV)

Meditation guidance

- **Take notice** of any areas of tension in your body. Relax your shoulders. Hold your hands palm up.

- **Be attentive** to your breath. Breathe naturally. Repeat the words from this scripture with each breath.

  As you breathe in say: *Search me,* and as you breathe out say: *Lord.* From Psalm 139:23 (NIV)

- **Redirect** your thoughts back to the phrase, *Search me, Lord..* Take notice of what where your wandering thoughts want to take you.

Listening to your heavenly Father

Listening to God. Now that your heart has been searched by the Holy Spirit, listen to what God is saying about the condition of your heart and the wandering thoughts that fill your mind.

Love the LORD your God, listen to his voice, and hold fast to him. Deuteronomy 30:20 (NIV)

Meditation guidance

- **Take notice** of what God is teaching you about your thoughts, attitude and relationships with other people.

  Show me your ways, LORD, teach me your paths. Psalm 25:4 (NIV)

- **Be attentive** to anything unclean in your heart—hard areas of your heart that are like knots in the shoulders.

  And He [the Holy Spirit], when He comes, will convict the world concerning sin. John 16:8 (NASB)

- **Concentrate on** understanding why you need to repent before God, and change your attitude and behavior. Work to remove these hard knots from your heart.

Leaving God's Throne Room

Your heavenly Father's guidance. God promises that he will guide you. As you leave your heavenly Father's throne room, meditate on God's will concerning the direction in which he wants to take you.

The Lord will guide you continually, giving you water when you are dry and restoring your strength. You will be like a well-watered garden, like an ever-flowing spring. Isaiah 58:11 (NLT)

Meditation guidance

- **Reflect on** God's wisdom and guidance, freely given to all his children. Meditate on these words:

  Have two goals: wisdom—that is, knowing and doing right—and common sense. Proverbs 3:21 (TLB)

- **Meditate on** the things that are pleasing to God.

  Do not be wise in your own eyes; fear the Lord and shun evil. This will bring health to your body and nourishment to your bones. Proverbs 3:7-8 (NIV)

- **Ask** your heavenly Father to guide you in your relationships and in the way you should live—your thoughts, words, and actions with others—so that they are acceptable to him.

  Direct my footsteps according to your word; let no sin rule over me. Psalm 119:133 (NIV)

IN THE ZONE

Make a list of people you want to intercede for on a regular basis. This could include your spouse and children, extended family members, godchildren, friends, work colleagues, church leaders and other believers. Select one or two people for each day of the month.

If necessary, use one of the earlier workouts to practice praying for yourself first, and then pray for other people. Think of it like the instructions given on airplanes that tell you to put your own oxygen mask on first. When you've prayed for yourself, then you can be more effective in interceding for other people.

Read my experience of praying for my cousin in Prayer Zone Journal Day 5.

Prayer Zone Journal Day 5

Pollution

October 25 - Duration: 39:26 minutes - Start time: 7:37 a.m. - End time: 8:16 a.m.

Pace: 16:16/mile - Distance: 2.43 miles - Calories: 193

Today, I begin my prayer time by praying for my cousin and his wife. Yet, a few minutes into this task, my mind wanders to thinking about his mother, who is my aunt, and my sister, who told me about a recent conversation she had with my aunt. For most of the lap I am lost in a mass of tangled thoughts regarding my aunt and sister. My cousin has been neglected!

I direct my mind back to prayer: *Search me...Lord,* I repeat rhythmically with each breath. *Why am I so bothered about this relationship?* It occurs to me that this concern is nothing new. It's often at the forefront of my mind. Then on the next lap it comes to me—I am *jealous.* My thoughts are consumed by my sister and aunt because I'm imagining the warm relationship they have developed since my mother died. I am *envious* of what they have and, not only that, I feel that I *deserve* the same. Then, another thought rises from deep within me—I *have a right to* enjoy an even better relationship with my aunt than my sister does.

Jealousy does not belong in the life of a child of God. Scripture says that being jealous is a sin.[1] However, my jealousy does not want to give up easily. I cross my arms, stamp my foot, and sulk, *"It's not fair!"* I feel entirely justified in my feelings. Jealousy is an unyielding knot within my heart.

Jealousy brings disorder in life.[2] It is not just an inward pollution of the heart but an outward poisoning of relationships. I think about two sisters in scripture, Leah and Rachel, whose relationship was marred by envy. Leah resented the love that Rachel received from their husband, and Rachel coveted Leah's fertility. Jealousy contributed to much pain and misery in their lives

I don't want to ruin the relationship with my sister. I don't want to displease you, either. If I am to have a healthier heart, jealousy has to go,

---

1   You are jealous of one another and quarrel with each other. Doesn't that prove you are controlled by your sinful nature? Aren't you living like people of the world? 1 Corinthians 3:3 (NLT)

2   Whenever people are jealous or selfish, they cause trouble and do all sorts of cruel things. James 3:16 (CEV)

I continue to ponder these thoughts for two more laps, allowing myself a few more stomps of the feet, and self-pity, but eventually, I realize it is time to hand over the matter to God. I need to repent.

Journal Reflecition

Does your mind wander when you pray? Do you interpret this as a lack of concentration and inability to stay focused, or as a failure to pray well?

Have you considered taking the time to investigate your thoughts—to take them captive and turn them into prayer? As 2 Corinthians 10:5 (NIV) says: *We demolish arguments and every pretension that sets itself up against the knowledge of God, and we take captive every thought to make it obedient to Christ.* Be encouraged that in this way, you are praying about *everything*, as scripture instructs.

Take notice of *where* your mind wanders when you pray. Have you discovered, through the help of the Holy Spirit, a knot in your heart, something that is making your heart hard? This may be anger, bitterness, jealousy, arrogance, or selfishness—something that doesn't fit with a life that is being conditioned by the Holy Spirit and made healthier.

Remember that even though the discovery of this knot may be a shock to you, it is not to God. He knows the deepest secrets of your heart.

Have you started to think of your spiritual heart being a muscle like your physical heart? Remember that God replaced your heart of stone with a heart of flesh. A heart of stone cannot have knots in it, but a heart of flesh can and does. So, don't be discouraged if your heart seems to be full of knots. Allow God, through his Holy Spirit, to massage your heart to be soft and pleasing to him.

Be encouraged that this workout *is* improving the health and fitness of your heart. The discovery of sin is an important step in this, but the next step is to do something about it.

Go to Prayer Zone Workout 6 if you need to repent and ask God for forgiveness.

Prayer is permitting the
potter to shape your heart.

Prayer Zone Workout 6

During Prayer Zone Workout 6 you will be using the prayer exercise below with your chosen physical exercise.

Use this prayer exercise when you are seeking God's forgiveness. No matter how difficult this may be, remember that you have a loving and merciful God who does not want to condemn you for your sin, but to free you from it.

This prayer exercise will give you an opportunity to pray for up to thirty minutes within a thirty-minute physical workout. Read through and contemplate the guidance given in the prayer exercise and then follow the IN THE ZONE instructions.

Preparing for Prayer: In this workout you will

- Begin by focusing on God who is merciful to you;

- Practice talking to God and confessing your impure thoughts, unhealthy emotions, wrong motives, careless words or deeds;

- Practice receiving God's forgiveness; and

- Finish today's exercise being encouraged to continue running the race of faith.

Entering God's Throne Room

A merciful God. Come confidently into the throne room of God, your Father. In God's presence, you receive his mercy. Reflect on the mercy that he gives.

So let us come boldly to the throne of our gracious God. There we will receive his mercy. Hebrews 4:16 (NLT)

Meditation guidance

- **Imagine** kneeling before the merciful God. Remember these words as you spend time in God's presence:

You are a gracious and merciful God. Nehemiah 9:31 (NIV)

- **Meditate on** knowing there is nothing you can do to deserve God's mercy. God's mercy is given freely and unconditionally. God takes pleasure in showering you with kindness and compassion.

For mercy is your specialty. That's what you love most. And compassion is on its way to us. Micah 7:18 (MSG)

- **Reflect on** God's mercy as his light shining on you, as you kneel before God's throne. Use this scripture to help you:

Because of God's tender mercy, the morning light from heaven is about to break upon us, to give light to those who sit in darkness and in the shadow of death, and to guide us to the path of peace. Luke 1:78-79 (NLT)

Talking to your heavenly Father

A heart that is dark. Do you acknowledge areas of your heart may be dark and unclean? In God's throne room, bring the impurity of your heart before your heavenly Father and Jesus Christ.

If we say that we share in life with God and keep on living in the dark, we are lying and are not living by the truth. 1 John 1:6 (CEV)

Meditation guidance

- **Talk to** God and tell him you accept the invitation through his son, Jesus, to bring the sin-sick areas of your life to him.

Jesus said: "Who needs a doctor: the healthy or the sick? I'm here inviting the sin-sick, not the spiritually fit." Mark 2:17 (MSG)

- **Speak to** your heavenly Father with honesty about specific unhealthy thoughts, emotions, motives, words and actions of your heart and life.

If we say that we have not sinned, we are fooling ourselves, and the truth isn't in our hearts. 1 John 1:8 (CEV)

- **Express** your desire to follow Jesus so that your heart will be filled with his light.

"I am the light of the world. Whoever follows me will never walk in darkness, but will have the light of life." John 8:12 (NIV)

Talking to your heavenly Father

Seeking forgiveness. Acknowledge wrongdoing and turn in repentance to God. Practice repenting for the unclean thoughts, words and actions in your heart and life.

I confess my sin to you, God. And I stop trying to hide my guilt.
Based on Psalm 32:5

Meditation guidance

- **Talk to** God about the sacrifice of his Son, Jesus Christ for your sins:

  Jesus said: "This is my blood.... It will be poured out, so that many people will have their sins forgiven." Matthew 26:28 (CEV)

- **Speak to** God about your desire for mercy. You sin against God, but it is at God's throne you receive mercy. Ask God for mercy.

  Have mercy on me, O God, because of your unfailing love. Because of your great compassion, blot out the stain of my sins. Wash me clean from my guilt. Purify me from my sin. Psalm 51:1-2 (NLT)

- **Express** your desire for forgiveness. Confess your wrongdoing.

  Lord; forgive me, for I have sinned against you. Based on Psalm 41:4

Listening to your heavenly Father

Receiving forgiveness. Your heavenly Father forgives when you repent. When you ask, you are forgiven. God does not remember your wrongdoing. Your heart is made pure.

But if we confess our sins to God, he will keep his promise and do what is right: he will forgive us our sins and purify us from all our wrongdoing. 1 John 1:9 (GNT)

Meditation guidance

• **Take notice** of what God says, now you have repented. Listen to his words:

I will forgive their wickedness, and I will never again remember their sins. Hebrews 8:12 (NLT)

• **Be attentive** to God's promise to remove your guilt. Listen to these words:

Finally, I confessed all my sins to you and stopped trying to hide my guilt. I said to myself, "I will confess my rebellion to the Lord." And you forgave me! All my guilt is gone. Psalm 32:5 (NLT)

• **Concentrate on** delighting in your pure heart.

Though your sins are like scarlet, I will make them as white as snow. Though they are red like crimson, I will make them as white as wool. Isaiah 1:18 (NLT)

Leaving God's Throne Room

Running the race. As you leave your heavenly Father's throne room, reflect on your spiritual exercise and the fitness of your spiritual heart. Ask your heavenly Father to equip you with endurance and strength to continue the race of your life.

And let us run with perseverance the race marked out for us.
Hebrews 12:1 (NIV)

Meditation guidance

- **Reflect on** the witnesses that scripture talks about, those who have already run the race of faith, who are cheering you on.

  All these pioneers who blazed the way, all these veterans cheering us on? It means we'd better get on with it. Strip down, start running— and never quit! No extra spiritual fat, no parasitic sins. Hebrews 12:1 (MSG)

- **Meditate on** Jesus. Keep your eyes on him so that you do not get weary.

  Let us keep our eyes fixed on Jesus, on whom our faith depends from beginning to end. Hebrews 12:2 (GNT)

- Ask God to give you strength, endurance, and patience.

  We also pray that you will be strengthened with all his glorious power so you will have all the endurance and patience you need. Colossians 1:11 (NLT)

IN THE ZONE

Do not be fearful of the work that your heart may need. Remember that your heavenly Father is like a potter who *gently* forms you into an object of beauty.

Are you embarrassed, surprised, or even shocked by what you need to repent? Remember that nothing is a surprise or shock to your heavenly Father. He knows everything about you. Be open to the Holy Spirit's searching and to your heavenly Father's work on your heart.

Forgiveness from God, through his Son, Jesus, is guaranteed. Do you have difficulty accepting this? Are you forgiving yourself? If you are not, ask God to help you move on.

Scripture says that God forgets your wrongdoing. However, it may be hard for you to forget. Now that you are familiar with this method of praying, practice an additional five minutes of breath prayer during your workout to help you focus on the positive rather than the negative. Use these words: *You are my rock and redeemer.* (Psalm 19:14 NIV)

Read my experience of praying for mercy in Prayer Zone Journal Day 6.

Prayer Zone Workout Journal: Day 6

Mercy Words

December 2 - Duration: 31:29 minutes - Start time: 7:35 a.m. - End time: 8:06 a.m. - Pace: 16:09/mile - Distance: 1.95 miles - Calories: 155

This morning I try to understand God's mercy. Unfortunately, my mind is distracted by a multitude of daily tasks. I am tempted to cut short my Prayer Zone Workout, but I decide to walk one more lap, contemplating the mystery of mercy. I repeat: *Lord, have mercy on me.*

It's impossible to stay standing while asking God for mercy. In my imagination, I fall on my knees before the steps leading to God's throne. I bow my head: *Lord, have mercy on me.*

Every word in that phrase is loaded.

I begin with the last word: *me.* I see myself wearing a long bridal train that is the stuff of my life. In areas, it is dull, grubby and unattractive. It's heavy, too. With determination, I yank it through the entrance pillars leading to God's throne room. *What a ridiculously comical sight,* I think to myself. The intricate lacework representing the details of my life are draped around me, displayed for God's attention—every action, thought, and spoken word. *I come before you to seek your mercy. Please, accept me and show compassion toward all my thoughts, words, and deeds.* I am amazed the holy God doesn't throw me, with my stained and soiled train, from his presence.

Asking for and receiving mercy requires each of us, actually or figuratively, to kneel before God and recognize him as *Lord,* the first word in the phrase *Lord, have mercy on me.* It is not just with my lips that I profess God as Lord, but with my heart, too. Kneeling symbolizes my heartfelt conviction that I am not worthy of God's mercy. The imperfect bridal train spreads out on the throne room floor as I worship. God's mercy billows forth from him and fills the temple. I am swathed in his greatness, power, strength, purity, majesty, holiness, and mercy. *Lord,* my heart speaks again,,recognizing that God is the lord of my life, embracing me but separate from and greater than me.

God desires a contrite heart. This is what I give to him on the fifth lap, the one I almost didn't complete.

Have mercy on me, O God, according to your unfailing love;
according to your great compassion... My sacrifice, O God, is a
broken spirit; a broken and contrite heart you, God, will not
despise. Psalm 51:1, 17 (NIV)

The low winter sun rises higher from behind the trees with each lap I complete. Bare branches cast long shadows the length of the track. It is cold in the shade, but the sun is moving on its westward course, and on the next lap, it emerges full and bright. I am bathed in sunlight. My body is released from the chilly grip of a cold December morning. God's mercy, like the sun, warms my soul.

God's greatness doesn't require me to remain submissive. With the words *have mercy*, I ask the heavenly Father to bring forth his tenderness and compassion. He answers those words, *have mercy*, by showing me favor, and the outpouring of his grace.

I complete four laps beyond my normal routine. It's a physical accomplishment, but more significantly, my imaginary train has been transformed. It gleams brightly as I leave the track to tackle another new day.

Journal Reflection

How do you understand God's mercy?

Do you know that despite our unworthiness, God refuses to wash his hands of us? Instead he shows compassion and loving kindness to us. Ephesians 2:4 says *God is rich in mercy.*

Mercy is an expression of his love. It is God's mercy that saves us.

Prayer is asking for mercy and receiving purity.

Prayer Zone Workout 7

During Prayer Zone Workout 7 you will be using the prayer exercise below with your chosen physical exercise.

Use this prayer exercise when you are hurting, particularly from the words or actions of other people. Use it as an opportunity to do what is often not easy—to pray for people who give you a hard time. However, this exercise also allows you to bring to God any anger or bitterness regarding the person or persons who have hurt you.

This exercise will give you an opportunity to pray for twenty-five minutes while completing a twenty-five minute physical workout. Read through and contemplate the guidance given in the prayer exercise and then follow the IN THE ZONE instructions.

Preparing for Prayer. In this workout you will

- Begin by focusing on your heavenly Father who cares deeply for you;

- Practice praying about and for your "enemies;" as instructed by scripture, including talking to your heavenly Father about the suffering you are experiencing;

- Practice listening to God's promises to heal you and bring about justice; and

- Finish today's workout being reminded that your heavenly Father protects you.

Entering God's Throne Room

Your heavenly Father cares for you. God is tender and compassionate toward his children. Contemplate your heavenly Father's care for you.

And even the very hairs of your head are all numbered. So don't be afraid. Matthew 10:30-31 (NIV)

Meditation guidance

- **Imagine** God's knowledge of you, a knowledge that is far more intimate than any other person who knows you.

  You know when I am resting or when I am working, and from heaven you discover my thoughts. You notice everything I do and everywhere I go. Before I even speak a word, you know what I will say. Psalm 139:2-4 (CEV)

- **Meditate on** your value to God, your Father.

  Consider the ravens: They do not sow or reap, they have no storeroom or barn; yet God feeds them. And how much more valuable you are than birds! Who of you by worrying can add a single hour to your life? Luke 12:24-25 (NIV)

- **Reflect on** the good gifts that your heavenly Father gives to you.

  Which of you, if your son asks for bread, will give him a stone? Or if he asks for a fish, will give him a snake? If you, then, though you are evil, know how to give good gifts to your children, how much more will your Father in heaven give good gifts to those who ask him? Matthew 7:9-11 (NIV)

Talking to you heavenly Father

A heart that is hurting. Talk to God about the pain you are experiencing that is caused by other people. Then follow the instruction of scripture to "pray for those who persecute you."[1]

When someone gives you a hard time, respond with the energies of prayer. Matthew 5:44 (MSG)

Meditation guidance

- **Talk to** God about the pain and suffering you are experiencing because of those who have wronged you or caused you to suffer injustice.

  How long must I endure trouble? How long will sorrow fill my heart day and night? Psalm 13:2 (GNT)

- **Speak to** your heavenly Father about your feelings towards these individuals—even if what you are feeling is hatred. He knows anyway. Bring your anger and bitterness to God. Read how the Psalmist expresses his anger:

  When those thugs try to knife me in the back, make them look foolish. Frustrate all those who are plotting my downfall. Make them like cinders in a high wind, with God's angel working the bellows. Make their road lightless and mud-slick, with God's angel on their tails. Psalm 35:4-6 (MSG)

- **Express** any anger you feel towards God. Be honest with God. Then make a commitment not to stay angry.

  In your anger do not sin: Do not let the sun go down while you are still angry, and do not give the devil a foothold. Ephesians 4:26-27 (NIV)

---

1   Matthew 5:44 (NIV)

Listening to your heavenly Father

Receiving healing. In God's throne room, bring your wounded heart to your heavenly Father for healing. Remember, your heavenly Father cares for those who are hurting and suffering, and God brings justice for those unfairly treated.

The Lord works righteousness and justice for all the oppressed.
Psalm 103:6 (NIV)

Meditation guidance

- **Take notice** of your breathing as you reflect on Jesus' own suffering.

  ...a man who suffered, who knew pain firsthand. Isaiah 53:3 (MSG)

- **Be attentive** to your heavenly Father's healing hands.

  He heals the brokenhearted and binds up their wounds. Psalm 147:3 (NIV)

- **Concentrate on** your breathing and ask your heavenly Father to heal your mind, heart and life.

  As you breathe in say: *Relieve the troubles of my heart* and as you breathe out say: *free me from my anguish.* Psalm 25:17 (NIV)

Talking to your heavenly Father

Forgiving others. God has forgiven you. Therefore, he asks that you forgive others. In God's throne room, talk to your heavenly Father about the people you need to forgive.

> *But when you are praying, first forgive anyone you are holding a grudge against, so that your Father in heaven will forgive your sins, too.* Mark 11:25 (NLT)

Meditation guidance

- **Talk to** God about the forgiveness you receive from him.

- **Give** God about the resentment, bitterness, or anger you still feel toward the person you should forgive.

> *Peter came up to the Lord and asked, "How many times should I forgive someone who does something wrong to me? Is seven times enough?" Jesus answered: "Not just seven times, but seventy-seven times!"* Matthew 18:21-22 (CEV)

- **Forgive** those who have wounded you. This can be difficult, and it can take a long time. Remember that God is infinitely patient with you.

> *The Lord is slow to anger and filled with unfailing love, forgiving every kind of sin and rebellion.* Numbers 14:18 (NLT)

Leaving God's throne room

Your heavenly Father protects you. God, your heavenly Father, promises to protect you. He will always keep you safe. As you leave God's throne room, focus on your heavenly Father's promise of safekeeping.

Whoever trusts in the Lord is kept safe. Proverbs 29:25 (NIV)

Meditation guidance

- **Reflect on** these words about God, who gives you protection:

  Won't God protect his chosen ones who pray to him day and night? Won't he be concerned for them? He will surely hurry and help them. Luke 18:7-8 (CEV)

- **Meditate on** these words as you prepare to leave the security of your heavenly Father's throne room:

  But blessed are those who trust in the Lord and have made the Lord their hope and confidence. They are like trees planted along a riverbank, with roots that reach deep into the water. Such trees are not bothered by the heat or worried by long months of drought. Their leaves stay green, and they never stop producing fruit. Jeremiah 17:7-8 (NLT)

- **Tell** your heavenly Father that you trust him for the protection that you need as you go into your daily life. Repeat these words of scripture:

  You are my place of safety and my shield. Psalm 119:114 (CEV)

IN THE ZONE

When you are hurt, do you talk to a friend who cares and can give you support? Do you know that you can run to God for the same reason? Use this prayer exercise to practice coming to your heavenly Father who promises to care for you and protect you.

Isn't it better to pour out strong feelings to your heavenly Father, who knows what you are feeling, rather than "gossiping" with a friend?

Have you ever expressed to God—who knows your deepest thoughts and the secrets of your heart—your true feelings about the person who is hurting you? Bring the strong emotions you are experiencing to him. However, be aware that this place of pain and anger is not where you should stay.

What is your reaction to praying for your enemies and "those who persecute" you? Is your answer that you cannot, or will not, pray for them? What are your reasons? Perhaps you think they do not deserve to be shown God's favor or receive his forgiveness. Do you think they deserve punishment instead of God's goodness?

God's purpose is for all people to come to know the truth about him and be saved.[2] Can you see this as one purpose to pray for the people who hurt you?

Read my experience of praying when I was hurting in Prayer Zone Journal Day 7.

---

2   For God so loved the world that he gave his one and only Son, that whoever believes in him shall not perish but have eternal life. For God did not send his Son into the world to condemn the world, but to save the world through him. John 3:16 (NIV)

Prayer Zone Workout Journal: Day 7

Wounded

October 18 - Duration: 30:36 minutes - Start time: 7:33 a.m. - End time: 8:04 a.m.
Pace: 16:00/mile - Distance: 1.91 miles - Calories: 152

This morning I feel the pain of a freshly wounded heart. The lacerations come on top of older injuries inflicted by the same "friend" this year. I mull over her previous attacks, which reach me even when we talk on the phone. That first time I didn't see it coming. I had no idea. It hurt so much. *Did I deserve it?* I recall the words that whipped like a knife across my heart. No wonder I stepped back. Anyone would cool in a relationship after that.

Things got better, but not for long. I got closer and within striking distance again. I can hear the words that stung me a second time.

The track becomes a blur. I wipe my eyes. *Why do I continue to be kind and considerate? Why don't I just walk away, never to be hurt again? I step so cautiously, trying not to provoke, and she just lashes out at me. Is it my fault? Why has it happened again?*

I hate her. God, how can you love her? I can give as good as I get. Yeah, I can make her miserable, too. Yet anger is a poor guard for my battered and bruised heart.

I tire from the emotional trauma. With slower steps I ask: *heal my wounds and the pain. Help me move on. But, how? I cannot easily walk away from this relationship. Protect me from getting hurt again. I don't want to be a victim again. I hurt. I want things to be better. I love her, really.*

I limp around the track. I imagine Jesus, sleeves rolled up, squatting in front of me, a pile of bandages beside him, washing and binding my wounds with his gentle hands. When he was on earth, people came to him and were healed. I sigh. If only I could recover so easily.

I imagine my "enemy" standing with me before God's throne. I don't want her there, even though she is a child of God. My anger may have subsided, but it's going to take time for love and forgiveness to take its place.

Journal Reflection

Are you hurting from a difficult relationship? Your Prayer Zone Workout is a healthy way to deal with your emotions. Praying is the best way to release pent up emotions. Physical exercise will help relieve the stress that can cause you to be angry.

Wounds can run deep. You may need to spend more than one workout praying and receiving the tender care of your heavenly Father to experience healing.

If you are in a place of danger in a relationship, do not stay in harm's way. Seek professional help.

Prayer is healing our hurts.

Prayer Zone Workout 8

During Prayer Zone Workout 8 you will be using the prayer exercise below with your chosen physical exercise.

This prayer exercise is to help you resist temptation and attacks of the spiritual enemy. Although temptations and attacks are intended to turn you away from living a life with God, this exercise helps you stand firm in faith and enables you to rely on the riches God supplies to meet all your needs.

This exercise will give you an opportunity to pray for twenty-five minutes while completing a twenty-five minute physical workout. Read through and contemplate the guidance given in the prayer exercise and then follow the IN THE ZONE instructions.

Preparing for Prayer: In this part of your workout you will

- Begin by focusing on the inheritance and riches you receive from your heavenly Father;

- Practice talking to God about the temptations you face. In particular you will talk to God about the urge to turn away from him when life is difficult;

- Practice recognizing and resisting attack from the flaming arrows of the spiritual enemy;

- Finish today's workout putting on the armor of God and taking up the shield of faith that will protect you.

Entering God's Throne Room

Coming into an inheritance. Your heavenly Father has a rich inheritance for you. He provides a glorious and perfect future inheritance, and he showers you with riches and blessings today.

And we have a priceless inheritance—an inheritance that is kept in heaven for you, pure and undefiled, beyond the reach of change and decay. 1 Peter 1:4 (NLT)

Meditation guidance
- **Imagine** standing before the king of heaven and earth. As a child of God, you are his heir:

  And if you are a child, you're also an heir, with complete access to the inheritance. Galatians 4:7 (MSG)

- **Meditate on** God's riches available to you now. Consider how God gives you

  Strength: *I pray that out of his glorious riches he may strengthen you with power through his Spirit in your inner being.* Ephesians 3:16 (NIV)

  Hope: *I pray that your hearts will be flooded with light so that you can understand the confident hope he has given to those he called—his holy people who are his rich and glorious inheritance.* Ephesians 1:18 (NLT)

  Wisdom and understanding: *All the richest treasures of wisdom and knowledge are embedded in that mystery [Jesus Christ] and nowhere else.* Colossians 2:3 (MSG)

- **Reflect on** your heavenly Father's desire to make certain all your needs are met.

  And with all his abundant wealth through Christ Jesus, my God will supply all your needs. Philippians 4:19 (GNT)

Talking to your heavenly Father

Turning toward God. Talk to God about the temptation to turn away from him, particularly if life is hard and you do not feel that God is meeting all your needs.

Yet not my will, but yours be done. Luke 22:42 (NIV)

Meditation guidance:
- **Talk to** God about any struggle you may have accepting suffering in your life. Remember Jesus's own human struggle with doing the will of God, as experienced in the garden of Gethsemane.

  "Father, if you are willing, please take this cup of suffering away from me. Yet I want your will to be done, not mine."…He prayed more fervently, and he was in such agony of spirit that his sweat fell to the ground like great drops of blood. Luke 22:42, 44 (NLT)

- **Speak** about the temptation to turn away from God and go your own way.

  Jesus understands every weakness of ours, because he was tempted in every way that we are. But he did not sin! Hebrews 4:15 (CEV)

- **Express** your need for hope, wisdom, understanding, and strength. Remember God's promise to meet all your needs.

  Then an angel from heaven appeared and strengthened him [Jesus]. Luke 22:43 (NLT)

Listening to your heavenly Father

Removing enemy arrows. Your mind, heart and life are under constant attack from the flaming arrows of the enemy. This struggle is with spiritual powers opposed to God. Practice extinguishing and removing the arrows from your heart.

Extinguish all the flaming arrows of the evil one. Ephesians 6:16 (NIV)

Meditation guidance

- **Take notice** of, with the help of the Holy Spirit, enemy arrows lodged in your heart such as unhealthy desires and passions, anger, hatred, bitterness, revenge and greed—things that may lead to other sin.

  Don't grieve God. Don't break his heart. His Holy Spirit, moving and breathing in you, is the most intimate part of your life, making you fit for himself. Don't take such a gift for granted. Make a clean break... Ephesians 4:30-31 (MSG)

- **Be attentive** to removing any flaming arrows lodged in your heart.

  Therefore, get rid of... the evil that is so prevalent and humbly accept the word planted in you, which can save you. James 1:21 (NIV)

- **Concentrate on** breathing and resisting the arrows of the enemy. Follow Jesus's example and say:

  Go away, Satan! The scripture says, worship the Lord your God and serve only him! Matthew 4:10 (GNT)

Leaving God's throne room

Guarding your heart. Practice putting on the armor provided by God to guard your heart, and your mind, and your life. Use it to protect you against the flaming arrows of enemy attack.

Above all else, guard your heart, for everything you do flows from it. Proverbs 4:23 (NIV)

Meditation guidance

- **Reflect on** each part of the armor that protects you. Imagine being dressed in the armor of God—truth, righteousness, peace, faith, and salvation.

Stand your ground, putting on the belt of truth and the body armor of God's righteousness. For shoes, put on the peace that comes from the Good News so that you will be fully prepared. In addition to all of these, hold up the shield of faith to stop the fiery arrows of the devil. Put on salvation as your helmet, and take the sword of the Spirit, which is the word of God. Ephesians 6:14-17 (NLT)

- **Meditate on** the inner strength and courage that God provides through his Holy Spirit.

I ask God from the wealth of his glory to give you power through his Spirit to be strong in your inner selves. Ephesians 3:16 (GNT)

- **Concentrate on** standing firm in your faith in God. Be attentive and on guard.

Keep vigilant watch over your heart; that's where life starts....
Watch your step, and the road will stretch out smooth before you.
Proverbs 4:23, 26 (MSG)

Leaving God's Throne Room

The shield of faith. As you leave your heavenly Father's throne room and go out into your daily life, arm yourself with the shield of faith to deflect the arrows of the enemy.

> *... hold up the shield of faith to stop the fiery arrows of the devil.*
> Ephesians 6:16 (NLT)

Meditation guidance

- **Reflect on** using the shield of faith to resist the arrows of the enemy during your day.

- **Meditate on** your faith in God and ask God to strengthen your faith.

  Be on your guard; stand firm in the faith; be courageous; be strong.
  Do everything in love. 1 Corinthians 16:13-14 (NIV)

- **Tell** God you want to keep sin from your heart. Ask God to help you block and resist the ungodly things that you hear and see during the day.

  If I had cherished sin in my heart, the Lord would not have
  listened; but God has surely listened and has heard my prayer.
  Psalm 66:18-19 (NIV)

IN THE ZONE

Colossians 3:2 (NIV) says: *Set your heart on things above, not earthly things.* How often do you think or pray about the future inheritance you have as a child of God?

During the warm-up in this exercise, meditate on how God gives riches now: strength—in your inner being, hope—by flooding your heart with light, wisdom and understanding—through Jesus Christ. Remember that your Prayer Zone Workouts allow you to practice receiving all these riches.

Have you thought about life as a spiritual battle? Ephesians 6:12 (CEV) says: *We are not fighting against humans. We are fighting against forces and authorities and against rulers of darkness and powers in the spiritual world.* Knowing this, will you think about your struggles in life and with other people differently? Often the enemy uses other people to attack us. Do you need to get better at recognizing the origin of these arrows?

God promises to supply all your physical and spiritual needs. In your prayers, are you inclined to focus on your physical needs more than your spiritual needs?

In ancient times, soldiers stood in line and together their shields would form a defense against enemy arrows. Are you standing alone or with other people of faith?

Remember that the scripture verses you use in these prayer exercises are also part of your armor—*the sword of the Spirit.* Print out scripture verses from the Prayer Zone Workout web site or write them down and carry them with you during your workout. Try to memorize one or two scriptures to use when you are under attack.

Read my experience of standing firm in my battle with cancer in Prayer Zone Journal Day 8.

Prayer Zone Workout Journal: Day 8

Standing firm in my armor

February 3 - Duration: 18:40 minutes - Start time: 7:32 a.m. - End time: 7:51 a.m.

Pace: 17:03/mile - Distance: 1.09 miles - Calories: 87

My mind dwells on the latest news from the hospital following my recent MRI—another suspect lump. *I asked for no more bad things to happen. I can't handle anything more.* I need one more biopsy. *Will it be cancerous?* I suspect so.

The motion of walking the track brings some relief to my troubled thoughts.

I do not want to go through another biopsy. It makes me feel like a slab of meat—laid out on the table, prodded, squashed, needles inserted, bits extracted. I conveyed this image to my son: "Mom, you need to start worrying when they [the doctors] bring out the salt and pepper." We laughed, for a moment. *Now I have to go through it all again.* I stretch my neck from side to side. The muscles feel taut like violin strings, except they would not give sweet music.

I'm at the track to pray yet my heart is turned away from God.

Why did this happen? Why didn't you answer my prayer?

An arrow burns in my heart—doubt. Today, I doubt God's goodness. I doubt his care for me. *Have you abandoned me?* I feel alone. I doubt God's ability to provide for me. The arrowhead festers in my heart.

Help me in my unbelief.

Help me remove this arrow. I imagine pulling it from my heart. *I need faith in you.*

"Above all else, guard your heart, because it is the key to life," I'm a sloppy guard of the castle of my heart. My drawbridge is down, the portcullis is up, and the gates are wide open. I'm not prepared. I usually don't recognize my attacker!

Do not give the devil a foothold.[1]

I turn to God on his throne. There is no fear of attack in his throne room. Yet, I need protection when I leave.

I imagine the royal courtiers of God, his angels, dressing me in the ar-

---

1   Ephesians 4:27

mor that my heavenly Father provides. God's truth, like a thick belt, is tied around my waist. Righteousness—not my own self-righteousness, but the righteousness of God—protects my chest and back. A helmet reminds me I am saved through Jesus Christ. I slip my feet into shoes of peace. I pick up the shield that is faith; and the sharp sword of scripture.

I am dressed like a knight ready for battle, ready to defend the castle of my heart. Now, I'm on high alert, ready to resist the attacker.

I imagine this easily, but I have to admit: armor is difficult to wear. *I need to practice more.* It feels clumsy. *How am I going to manage?*

Stand firm, then says the instructions. I am relieved; I only have to stand.

Protected on the outside, I have your Spirit on the inside. I breathe in his Spirit as I come down the final straight and leave the track.

Journal Reflection

Scripture reminds us that God is good, yet we live in a world of good and evil.

How do you react to God when bad things happen? Do you blame God?

Do you need to remember that your battle is with the spiritual powers of darkness and evil, and not with God?

Prayer is our first line of defense.
(Oswald Chambers)

Prayer Zone Workout 9

During Prayer Zone Workout 9 you will be using the prayer exercise below with your chosen physical exercise.

This prayer exercise is an opportunity to give thanks to God. Sometimes, when you are in the middle of a crisis or everything seems to be going wrong, it is hard to be thankful. This exercise is to help you be thankful for even the smallest of things. When life is going well, this prayer exercise guides you to direct your thanks and praise to God.

This exercise will give you an opportunity to pray for twenty-five minutes while completing a twenty-five minute physical workout. Read through the prayer exercise and then follow the IN THE ZONE instructions.

Preparing for Prayer: In this part of your workout you will

- Begin by reflecting on your adoption into God's family.

- Practice talking to God about the extent of your thankfulness.

- Practice listening to the Holy Spirit and discover what you can be thankful for. You will follow this by expressing thanks to God. This is your interval training.

- Finish today's workout thanking God, no matter how small this may be and directing thanks to him throughout your day and in a more public setting within the family of God.

Entering God's Throne Room

Adopted by God. Come into God's throne room as his adopted child. Belief in Jesus Christ brings about your adoption, and God's Holy Spirit confirms your adoption.

God's Spirit touches our spirits and confirms who we really are. We know who he is and we know who we are: Father and children.
Romans 8:16 (MSG)

Meditation guidance

- **Imagine** your adoption into God's family. It is through belief in Jesus Christ that God adopts you as his child. Meditate on knowing that you are a child of God and that he dearly loves you.

  To all who believed him (Jesus Christ) and accepted him, he gave the right to become children of God. They are reborn—not with a physical birth resulting from human passion or plan, but a birth that comes from God. John 1:12-13 (NLT)

- **Meditate on** your standing as a child of God. Ask Abba to confirm in your heart that you are his child.

  You can tell for sure that you are now fully adopted as his own children because God sent the Spirit of his Son into our lives crying out, "Papa! Father!" Doesn't that privilege of intimate conversation with God make it plain that you are a child? Galatians 4:6 (MSG)

- **Reflect on** God being the father you do not have, if you are without an earthly father. If the relationship with your earthly father is broken, think about God, who offers the perfect fatherly relationship. Call out to your heavenly Father. Repeat his name: "Abba" or "Papa."

  A father to the fatherless...is God in his holy dwelling. Psalm 68:4-5 (NIV)

Talking to your heavenly Father

Being thankful. Focus on being thankful to God in all circumstances. Talk to your heavenly Father about your circumstances and particularly any lack of thankfulness.

And give thanks for everything to God the Father. Ephesians 5:20 (NLT)

Meditation guidance

- **Talk to** God about whether you feel ready to give thanks to him in the midst of your current circumstances.
- **Speak to** your heavenly Father about him guiding you to understand details of your life for which you can be thankful

  Ask God to fill you with the knowledge of his will, with all the wisdom and understanding that his Spirit gives. Colossians 1:9 (GNT)

- **Express** your belief in God that everything in your life is within your heavenly Father's care.

  I may walk through valleys as dark as death, but I won't be afraid. You are with me. Psalm 23:4 (CEV)

Listening to your heavenly Father

Breath prayer. Let your heart be examined by God's Spirit. Listen to discover whether there is something for which you can be thankful.

Speak, your servant is listening. 1 Samuel 3:10 (NLT)

Meditation guidance

- **Take** notice of any areas of tension in your body. Relax your shoulders. Hold your hands palm up.

- **Be attentive** to your breath. Breathe naturally. Repeat the words from this scriptures with each breath:

  As you breathe in say: *Speak,* and as you breathe out say: *Your servant is listening.* From 1 Samuel 3:10 (NLT)

- **Concentrate on** your thankfulness. Is God showing you something for which you should be giving thanks?

  I will give thanks to you, Lord, with all my heart; I will tell of all your wonderful deeds. Psalm 9:1 (NIV)

Talking to your heavenly Father

Giving thanks. Thank your heavenly Father for his goodness and for the good experiences and relationships in your life.

Give thanks to the Lord, for he is good. Psalm 106:1 (NIV)

Meditation guidance

- **Talk to** God about his goodness:

You are good, and what you do is good. Psalm 119:68 (NIV)

- **Speak words of** praise, worship, and thanksgiving. Join the royal household of your heavenly Father.

Enter his gates with thanksgiving and his courts with praise; give thanks to him and praise his name. Psalm 100:4 (NIV)

- **Express** thanks to God for the good in your life, no matter how small it might seem.

Whatever is good and perfect comes down to us from God our Father. James 1:17 (NLT)

Leaving God's throne room

Giving thanks. As you leave your heavenly Father's throne room, focus on giving thanks and glory to God in public.

With praise and thanksgiving they sang to the Lord. Ezra 3:11 (NIV)

Meditation guidance

- **Reflect on** how you can make giving thanks to God a reality in your day-to-day life. Ask God to help you give the credit to him for the good things in your life.

Our sacrifice is to keep offering praise to God in the name of Jesus. Hebrews 13:15 (CEV)

- **Meditate on** the public element of giving thanks to God. Plan to spend time with other people with whom you can give thanks to God.

They praised the Lord and gave thanks as they took turns singing: "The Lord is good!" Ezra 3:11 (CEV)

- **Tell** God you are thankful. Bring God a thanksgiving offering before you leave his throne room.

IN THE ZONE

In your current circumstances, do you find it difficult to give thanks to God? Use this prayer exercise to find one small way you can give thanks. Maybe you can be thankful for your adoption into God's family?

If you recognize the good quality of your current circumstances, then use this exercise to fully express your thankfulness to God. Take an additional step of giving God the credit for good things in your life by either expressing this to other people or take part in worshipping with other believers.

God is the source of all good things in life. This is easy to forget. When good things happen, you may give yourself or other people credit, rather than God. This exercise is to help you direct thanks and praise to the one who deserves them.

God's goodness is like his grace. It is underserved but freely given. Does this make you even more thankful?

Giving thanks to God in your personal prayer during your Prayer Zone Workout is the right thing to do, but scripture shows that there is a public element to giving thanks, too. Remember to give thanks to God in a more public way within the family of God, perhaps in corporate prayer or attending a worship service.

Read my experience of being thankful in Prayer Zone Journal Day 9.

Prayer Zone Journal: Day 9

A sparkling clean heart

June 7 - Duration: 38:08 minutes - Start time: 7:43 a.m. - End time: 8:26 a.m.

Pace: 19:54/mile - Distance: 1.92 miles - Calories: 147

I am God's adopted child. He reminded me of this the day my Dad died.

Today I am also reminded me that *everyone has sinned; we all fall short of God's glorious standard.* [1] I do not live up to God's expectations for his children.

I haven't been confessing lately. Confessing my wrongdoing before God is what scripture tells me to do. I continually mess up, yet today I can't think of any particular wrongdoing. Nothing sticks out in my mind. So, instead, I walk two laps practicing breath prayer: *Search me* I breathe in. *Your servant is listening*, I breathe out.

On the next lap I wait and listen. Still nothing comes to mind. *Maybe,* I think, *this part of my prayer exercise isn't working today.* It's a ridiculous thought. The Holy Spirit isn't like some magic genie who I conjure up. Neither is it that I don't have anything to confess at all. I'm far from perfect.

Instead, a line of a song comes to mind: *"I'm forgiven."* I can't remember the rest of the song. Yet, I hear the tune for that one line in my head. I sing it over and over again. *Is this what you want me to hear this morning?*

God doesn't always see my wrongdoing; he sees his child made pure and clean through Jesus' blood.

I am as white as snow.[2]

I am forgiven!

The track feels soft underfoot. My feet bounce on the surface.

I smile.

I don't always have to come with a plate full of sins to confess, like an offering to appease a god. Today, I bring an imaginary plate piled high with letters that read *"thank you."*

Thank you.

---

1   Romans 3:23 (NLT):.
2   Though your sins are like scarlet, they shall be as white as snow. Isaiah 1:18 (NIV)

Journal Reflection

If giving thanks to God is difficult to do, reflect on being a child of God, adopted into his family. You are forgiven, and you are washed clean. Give thanks for this during your Prayer Zone Workout.

Listen to the song *"You Are My King (Amazing Love)"* sung by Chris Tomlin, which contains the line: *I'm forgiven.*

Use your imagination when you give thanks to God. The Israelites brought thanksgiving offerings of bread and meat to the temple as a sign of devotion and thanks. [3] How can you creatively show in a physical way your thanks and devotion to God?

**Prayer is being grateful
even when life grates.**

---

3   Leviticus 7:11-15

Prayer Zone Workout 10

During Prayer Zone Workout 10 you will be using the prayer exercise below with your chosen physical exercise.

Use this prayer exercise to experience the peace and love of God in your heart and life.

This exercise will give you an opportunity to pray for twenty minutes while completing a twenty-minute physical workout. Read through and contemplate the guidance given in the prayer exercise and then follow the IN THE ZONE instructions.

Preparing for Prayer: In this workout you will

- Begin by making time to rest with God;

- Practice talking about the rest and peace that you need;

- Practice being filled with the Holy Spirit who provides peace and love in your heart; and

- Finish today's workout understanding the importance of these qualities for the health of your life and the benefit of other people.

Entering God's Throne Room

Find peace in God's presence. Come into your Father's throne room. Here you will find safety and peace. Focus on the gift of rest that God gives.

You've always given me breathing room, a place to get away from it all, a lifetime pass to your safe-house, an open invitation as your guest. Psalm 61:3-4 (MSG)

Meditation guidance

- **Imagine** walking with your heavenly Father during your workout. Reflect on God's invitation in this scripture passage:

Are you tired? Worn out? Burned out on religion? Come to me. Get away with me and you'll recover your life. I'll show you how to take a real rest. Walk with me and work with me—watch how I do it. Learn the unforced rhythms of grace. I won't lay anything heavy or ill-fitting on you. Keep company with me, and you'll learn to live freely and lightly. Matthew 11:28-30 (MSG)

- **Meditate on** the safety and peace that God, your Father, gives.

The Lord is my shepherd, I lack nothing. He makes me lie down in green pastures, he leads me beside quiet waters. Psalm 23:1-2 (GNT)

- **Reflect on** the one who provides peace in your life.

For you alone, Lord, make me dwell in safety. Psalm 4:8 (NIV)

Talking to your heavenly Father

Being still before God. Your heavenly Father offers you peace and rest. Talk to God about your ability to relax.

Come with me by yourselves to a quiet place and get some rest.
Mark 6:31 (NIV)

Meditation guidance:

- **Talk to** God about any restlessness you may feel. Contemplate God's words to you:

    Come to me, all you who are weary and burdened, and I will give you rest. Matthew 11:28 (NIV)

- **Speak** about your ability to cease striving—to:

    "Let go, relax, and know that I am God." Psalm 46:10 (NASB)

- **Express** your desire to live in peace with those around you.

    For the Kingdom of God is not a matter of what we eat or drink, but of living a life of goodness and peace and joy in the Holy Spirit. Romans 14:17 (NLT)

Listening to your heavenly Father

A pure and loving heart. It is the Holy Spirit who puts your desire for peace, and love for God and others in your heart. Practice allowing the Holy Spirit to fill your heart.

God has given us the Holy Spirit, who fills our hearts with his love. Romans 5:5 (CEV)

Meditation guidance
- **Take notice** of the work you have done to restore your heart. Repeat these words:

Who may stand in his holy place? Only those whose hands and hearts are pure. Psalm 24:3-4 (NLT)

- **Be attentive** to these words:

Blessed are the pure in heart, for they will see God. Matthew 5:8 (NIV)

- **Concentrate on** the Holy Spirit. Allow him to fill your heart.

But the fruit of the Spirit is love, joy, peace, forbearance, kindness, goodness, faithfulness, gentleness and self-control. Galatians 5:22-23 (NIV)

Leaving God's Throne Room

A healthy, overflowing heart. As you leave your heavenly Father's throne room, be determined to bring out the good stored in your heart so that it overflows into your life and the lives of other people.

A good man brings good things out of the good stored up in his heart. Luke 6:45 (NIV)

Meditation guidance

- **Reflect on** these healthy qualities—love, joy, peace, patience, self-control. Resolve to pursue them.

  Run after mature righteousness—faith, love, peace—joining those who are in honest and serious prayer before God. 2 Timothy 2:22 (MSG)

- **Meditate on** your intention to continue working towards a healthy and worthy life.

  Live a life worthy of the Lord and please him in every way: bearing fruit in every good work. Colossians 1:10 (NIV)

- **Tell** God you are single-minded about loving him and other people.

  Love the Lord your God with all your passion and prayer and muscle and intelligence—and...love your neighbor as well as you do yourself. Luke 10:27 (MSG)

IN THE ZONE

Up till now your Prayer Zone Workouts have had an inward focus and you have been working to improve the fitness and health of your spiritual heart. It is just as important to rest and find peace. This is good for you physically and spiritually. It benefits your life and the lives of other people. Do you feel at peace—that your workouts are improving your physical well-being and your spiritual health?

One of the purposes of looking after your spiritual health is so that others may know the truth about God through you. Are you ready to be life-changing for other people?

Read my experience of resting in God's presence in Prayer Zone Journal Day 10 below.

Prayer Zone Journal: Day 10

Finding Peace in God's Presence

October 20 - Duration: 40:40 minutes - Start time: 7:44 a.m. - End time: 8:24 a.m. - Pace: 16:30/mile - Distance: 2.46 miles – Calories: 196

My Prayer Zone Workout is like a sanctuary; a place of safety from all that the world throws at me. *You are my heavenly Father. You reign over everything in life.* Like the Psalmist, I say: *Let me live forever in your sanctuary, safe beneath the shelter of your wings.*[1]

I breathe deeply, exhaling my anxieties. *I rest in your presence.* I imagine stretching out on the throne room steps; I hope this doesn't sound too irreverent. I spend another whole lap relaxing on those steps. The sun is rising, in its same daily morning routine. *I am reminded of your faithfulness.* The leaves of the trees are changing color from green to red and orange as fall approaches. *Life changes like the seasons, but you God remain constant.* I sense God's dependable presence, and I am comforted.

I watch the other people exercising at the track. *God, you must have a sense of humor,* I think. Abraham jogs past. His name brings a smile to my face. *Is this for my amusement or to remind me of your presence?* For the God to whom I pray is the God of the ancient patriarch, Abraham. The Pink Apparition is at the track, too. Her exercise routine is entertaining. She alternates between jogging forward and backwards. I have never managed to catch up to the Pink Apparition, and she has never passed me. I'm intrigued to see what she looks like close up, but the hood of her pink sweatshirt hides her face. Another man strides up and down one side of the track. A long cane in his hands is extended horizontally over his head. Any type of exercise is acceptable. I love that. I wonder what my fellow track-mates would think of my spiritual exercise—relaxing on the steps to God's throne.

Heavenly Father, I have come here to be with you. I want to spend this time with you.

I see my favorite dog. He's a handsome fella, with a curly light-brown coat and the biggest black eyes. His master is walking him down the hill and across the road. He reaches the track, and then he stops and

---

1 Psalm 61:4 (NLT)

stands. Other dogs zigzag around and chase balls. However, this dog just stands peacefully. His owner waits patiently beside him. Today, I feel like this dog. I'm with my heavenly Father. We're spending time together.

Journal Reflection

Is the place where you go to exercise and pray your physical sanctuary? Somewhere that you can "get away from it all?" Is it a place where you can feel at peace and rest with your heavenly Father?

So often our prayers are full of requests. Every once in while, use this prayer exercise just to enjoy being in the presence of God, relaxing with him.

Mind/body therapies, such as the Relaxation Response developed by Dr. Herbert Benson[2], have scientifically proven that mental focus, as in prayer, and a passive attitude of putting aside distracting thoughts can bring enhanced states of well-being.[3] They can relieve headaches, reduce blood pressure among other benefits.[4] By combining the mental focus you are applying in these prayer exercises with the power of the Holy Spirit, *be encouraged* that you are on the road to better overall well-being.

Prayer is... resting in God's presence.

2   "Relaxation Response MGH," n.d., http://www.massgeneral.org/bhi/basics/rr.aspx.
3   Herbert Benson and Miriam Z. Klipper, *The Relaxation Response*, 1st Avon Books Printing, August 1976 edition (HarperTorch, 2000), xviii.
4   Herbert Benson, *Beyond the Relaxation Response: How to Harness the Healing Power of Your Personal Beliefs* (New York, N.Y.: Berkley Books, 1985), 5–6.

Conclusion

Your prayers… have been received by God as an offering. Acts
10:4 (NLT)

"We'll go shopping when I return," I called out to my daughter as I walked
out the door to head to the track for my Prayer Zone Workout. I smiled,
realizing that even though my daughter was home for school vacation, my
Prayer Zone Workout had not been derailed. Instead, my actions that day
demonstrated prayer coupled with exercise had become a priority, a daily
routine. Now my day functions around my workout rather than circumstances dictating whether or not I pray and exercise. And I knew that once
my workout was complete, my day with my daughter would go much better than if I'd not spent this time taking care of my body and my spiritual
heart.

You will remember it is rewards that keep us returning to practice a
behavior. Over the last few years, my rewards have been the gentle improve-
ments in spiritual heart health, which come from my practice of heart-talk.

I no longer run from intimate or frank conversation with my heavenly Father. Instead I hurry to include my heavenly Father in both the run-
of-the-mill activities and the extraordinary events of my life.

For years I grumbled and complained about living in New England
because it is not England, but bringing this protest to God now means I
take this fact of life in my stride.

I have covered mile after mile on the track agonizing over a difficult
relationship. Yet now the friendship is no longer fraught with antagonism.
Maybe my friend has had a change of heart. However, I know for certain
my heart has been changed. What God has healed in one tough relationship I know he can do again the next time another disagreement arises. So,
I keep coming back to prayer.

I channeled the despair of a diagnosis of breast cancer into walking
with my heavenly Father whenever my treatment would allow. I kept showing up at my special place even when my faith and trust in God seemed to
hang by a thread.

I regularly allow my heart to be searched and listen to what God has to say about unhealthy areas of my heart that without my Prayer Zone Workout time would go unnoticed.

Then, I ponder in amazement God's goodness and his grace shown to me, which I deserve no more than the next person.

My prayer for you is that through this book you will experience greater physical health, and deeper spiritual awareness, and that this inward sense of wholeness will be displayed outwardly as you make a positive difference in the world around you.

God receives your heart as an offering when you offer your heart through prayer.

Appendix 1

The smartphone app, Prayer Zone Workout, can be found on the companion website to this book at www.prayerzoneworkout.com. Simply visit the site from your iPhone, Android, or other smartphone device and get Prayer Zone Workout exercises to use on the go.

The app contains the prayer exercises from this book in condensed format, as well as additional exercises. The format makes them easy to use and refer to as you do your Prayer Zone Workout. Use them to guide your prayer.

In addition, the Prayer Zone Workout app contains a number of Starter Workouts. These consist of prayer exercises that have been preselected for you to form the prayer part of your workout, to help you as you establish your routine. Select a Starter Workout that fits your circumstances. The choices are:

When hurting
When repentant
When thankful
When in difficulty
For others
For peace
Your relationship with God

Appendix 2

Bible translations used in this book, and their abbreviations:

CEV	Contemporary English Version
GNT	Good News Translation
MSG	The Message
NASB	New American Standard Bible
NIV	New International Version (2011)
NLT	New Living Translation

Acknowledgments

Thank you to my husband, Colin, for your endless support and encouragement throughout the writing of this book. Thank you also for using your technical skills and contributing many hours of work to create the Prayer Zone Workout smartphone app and e-book. I could not have done this without you.

Thank you to my children: Phoebe, George, and Maximilian. You have encouraged me and been patient during the many hours I spent writing rather than attending to other things.

Thank you to Pen in Hand, the editing and coaching services of Eva Marie Everson, and my editor Janice Elsheimer. I have valued your excellent editing skills, insights, suggestions and encouragement to improve my writing. It has been a pleasure working with you and I look forward to meeting you in person one day.

Thank you to Jon Mullender for your awesome creative skills in designing the Prayer Zone Workout logo and book cover. How fantastic it was to work with my nephew on this project! And thank you to my niece, Emily Mullender, for giving up your summer to produce the Prayer Zone Workout videos and audio material.

Thank you to Kathryn Duprex for your enthusiastic feedback, and for being a good friend.

Thank you to Cynthia Fantasia, Pastor of Women at Grace Chapel, for being my friend, and for your support and direction. Thanks also to the Grace Chapel Women's Ministry prayer team for your many prayers.

Thank you to Dr. Steve Kang at Gordon-Conwell Theological Seminary for your insights and encouragement; and to the Reverend Dr. Moonjang Lee, whose course, The Practice of Prayer, motivated me to develop the more intentional prayer life that evolved into this book.

19100990R00085